HOPE

HOPE

I Will Fight Till The End

Maxine Mukuna

HOPE

HOPE

Published by

2/3/25

Be Blessed and Encouraged.

M. Mukhua
Maxine

HOPE

HOPE

Published in United Kingdom by Peaches Publications, 2019.

www.peachespublications.co.uk

The moral right of the author has been asserted.

All rights reserved. No part of this book may be reproduced, stored in a retrieval system, or transmitted in any form or by any means, electronic, mechanical, photocopying, recording, public performances or otherwise, without written permission of the publisher, except for brief quotations embodied in critical articles or reviews.

The right of Maxine Mukuna to be identified as the author of this work has been asserted in accordance with sections 77 and 78 of the copyright Designs and Patents Act 1988.

Text Copyright © 2019 by Maxine Mukuna.

British Library Cataloguing in Publication Data: A catalogue record for this book is available from the British Library.

ISBN: 978-0-244-35319-3

Book cover design: Peaches Publications.

Editor and Typesetter: Winsome Duncan.

Proofreader: Joanna Oliver.

HOPE

Contents

Dedication

Acknowledgements

Introduction

Chapters:

My Jewel, Ruby

My World Collapsed

Reality Used to be a Friend of Mine

The Final Block

The Last Lap

Unbreak My Heart

No Parent Should Have to Bury Their Child

New Normal

Hope, Glory and God

Scriptures and Prayers of Encouragement

Ten Favourite Songs

Epilogue

About the Author

Peaches Publications

Dedication

I dedicate this book in loving memory of my daughter, Ruby Asher Mukuna, who rests in peace after fighting a short battle with acute myeloid leukaemia.

Acknowledgements

First and foremost, I would like to thank God for taking me through this journey. Every day that I am alive is because of Christ's mercy and grace over my life. After Ruby died, I reached a point in life where I did not want to live. What was the point if I did not have my precious jewel, Ruby, by my side? Even in my darkest moments, God has kept me and for that, I am grateful.

Thank you to Dominique, who helped me to develop this book, to Jonathan, my Graphic Designer and to my publisher, Winsome Duncan at Peaches Publications, for helping me materialise my vision into a book.

To my wonderful parents, Clarinston and Pernella King, siblings Zena, Carol and Sharmaine, brother in laws, Rob and Shaun, all my nieces and nephews, aunties, uncles and other family members. My church family at Church of God of Prophecy, Small Heath and all my friends who have been a tower of strength. I would not have made it this far without you all.

I would also like to acknowledge all the staff who cared for Ruby from Birmingham Children's hospital and Macmillan Nurses. Also Edwards Trust counselling services, for their excellent support provided to me and the family and all those parents who were going through similar experience of bereavement and to this day still go through. Your care was amazing and it will never be forgotten.

It has not been easy, especially for my family. At the time, we had never experienced a loss of this magnitude. There were moments when they did not know what to say or do to make things better. At times the pain was so unbearable, nobody could help. This traumatic experience taught us all something; we learnt so much through our pain and how to heal the raw hurt left open in our wounds.

We lost a little person who captured our hearts and she is someone we will never forget, our precious GEM -

Ruby Asher Mukuna.

Introduction

In life there are days you will never forget and Sunday 9th July 2007, will be a day that I will never erase from my memory. On that painful day, as a family, we were informed that our precious GEM Ruby, was seriously ill and had been diagnosed with 'acute myeloid leukaemia'. What was that? Our family had never heard of this disease and now we would have to learn to live with it, now we will never forget it. Every time I hear the word leukaemia or cancer, it sends a shiver down my spine because I know first-hand what the treatment entails, especially for individuals who undergo chemotherapy treatment.

Thinking of my beautiful RUBY, knowing what her little body had to go through at such a tender age, she really was a unique child and such an inspiration.

My reason for writing this book, was inspired because throughout the period of her illness, she demonstrated courage and strength that I have never seen before. Ruby never gave up, even when I could see she was in so much pain, she would manage a smile for me but most of all she fought with all her might until the very end and she defied the doctor's expectations. Now I want the world to know her story.

HOPE

My precious jewel, Ruby, has given me HOPE that no matter what life throws at you, no matter how devastating the circumstances are and how hopeless you seem, with God, there is hope! Have faith. Be encouraged, know that with God, we can stand up. Yes, it may seem like we are in a battle but remember God is with us in every situation and at all times. God will never forsake us.

The fact that I am still standing is a sheer miracle and I bear witness to this story as a testament to God's love and mercy over my life. This very painful experience has been life changing. No parent should EVER have to bury their child. If I am honest, I don't like what I have had to go through but I am grateful because if I did not go through this experience, how could I write this book? How could I encourage others, especially parents, that there is HOPE?! It is my belief that God is our ROCK, our salvation and constant spring of living water, supplying us with everything that we need. HOPE in God enables us to move forward, it increases our faith, it lightens our darkness. Hope is healing and trusting that things will get better. There is a way out, so therefore we must take Ruby's example and keep fighting till the very end.

Here are five lessons that my little Ruby has taught me about life:

Lesson 1: To laugh, smile and giggle through the pain.

Lesson 2: That no matter what, never give up and always keep fighting.

Lesson 3: Be your authentic self and you have the right to make your own choice.

Lesson 4: Family is important.

Lesson 5: In life, things will not always look how they seem, always make an effort to pray against the prognosis or diagnosis.

My Jewel, Ruby

I remember it so well. On Friday 30th March 2006, I recall feeling uneasy whilst I sat on the bed. I felt extremely tired, in fact I had felt like that for a few days. I phoned my sister, Carol and explained my symptoms of extreme tiredness and exhaustion to her.

"Are you sure you're not pregnant?", Carol responded.

"Pregnant?", I laughed at her, as she likes to stir me up.

"Definitely not", I replied.

Then it dawned on me. Maybe she's right! I had a pregnancy test at home, as Ruby's dad and I had been married for three years and were trying for a baby at the time.

"Well, what else are you waiting for? Go and do the test and make sure you ring me back!", She urged.

I did as she requested. No one else was home at the time and I remember being in the bathroom. I remember waiting for the results. 'What if I am?', I thought. I so wanted a child of my own. I was used to being a mother-figure; a stepmother and an aunty to my nieces and nephew. 'Being pregnant would be incredible', I thought. I knew I would make a great mother. Two minutes went by. I remember being too scared, my eyes were closed. But I was also excited. I eventually gave in and opened it. There it was. The blue line with the word, 'pregnant'. Even then, I was in denial. No way! It must be wrong.

I phoned Carol back and took a deep breath.

"Well then?", she asked.

I announced the results and we both ended up laughing. "I'm going to be a mum"! I gasped. I had never felt so overwhelmed. Another chapter in my life was finally about to begin; one that I was looking forward to, of course. I was unaware of how short motherhood would be. I phoned Ruby's dad-to-be and he too was excited. Even though we were going through difficulties at the time, I knew this pregnancy would bring so much joy to us. I told my stepdaughter, my parents and my other sisters, Zena and Sharmaine. They were all overjoyed by the news.

As months passed, it became hard to tell I was actually pregnant. I believed Ruby was definitely a miracle baby sent by God. Pregnancy caused me no problems, apart from a urine infection. I sailed through it and only put on weight towards the end. I was still able to wear the same-size clothes, till at least six months. I had neither morning sickness nor cravings and even managed to travel abroad to Nevis, six months into my pregnancy. Thank you, Uncle William and Aunty Shirley, for spoiling me and ensuring I rested on the trip.

Birthed Out

On Saturday 18th November 2006, I was in agony. Luckily, my mum and Ruby's dad were with me at the time. I went to the hospital around midday and after being examined, they informed me that I was only 1cm dilated. I thought they were having a laugh! I was sent home and told to return when I was further dilated. I was not impressed and by 6.30 p.m., I returned. The contractions were unbearable at this point but I managed to get through it with the help of my new best friends, gas and air. My mum and Ruby's dad remained on the labour ward. I remember my mum at one point saying, "Maxine, you need to push."

"What do you think I'm doing?", I said, through the pain.

After going into the early hours of Sunday 19th November 2006, my GEM, Ruby, came into the world at 5.15 p.m. I remember waiting to hear her cry and she sure did. They placed her in my arms "What a GEM", I thought. Ruby's hair was so silky and long and she was so perfect in every way. All mothers believe their child is beautiful but MY RUBY was exceptionally beautiful. She was so innocent and precious. I knew that God had chosen me to be her mum. I was and still am, grateful for this golden opportunity of motherhood.

After several days in hospital, we both came home. It was difficult at first; my body adjusting, my emotions all over the place, entering a new unknown territory of being a mother. With my family's support, I eventually got into a routine. It became easier; they loved her dearly. My baby girl emanated warmth and joy. I remember being able to take her on holiday to Nevis with members of the church choir and family members. She loved Nevis so much, she splashed in the water and everyone she met loved her instantly. I did not know that this would be her first and last holiday. I thank God for this opportunity.

Sunday 8th April 2007, Ruby was almost five months old. We decided to get her christened. It was a very special day, as it was also Easter Sunday. The church was so full to the brim, some people had to stand! Another couple had their child christened on that day and now every time I see this child, he reminds me of Ruby. There is only a few months age difference.

HOPE

I always knew that I would call my daughter Ruby, her name means a rare 'precious jewel', or 'precious stone'. Her middle name, 'Asher', was chosen by one of her godparents. I remember Liela and I being at home one evening, trying to think of a middle name for her. Liela thought of 'Asher', so we decided to look up the meaning of this name: 'Happy or Blessed'. We all agreed that this was a name for Ruby because she truly was happy and blessed, without a doubt. I returned to work when Ruby was six months old. I didn't want to place her in nursery but I had no choice. The staff members really loved her, and she too loved them. She made such an impact in the short time she was there but that was Ruby all over. As soon as people laid eyes on her, they just fell in love with her. Even at six to seven months old, she had character. Her eyes were beautiful and big, she was like a Disney Princess. I know she got her beautiful looks from me of course. I loved being Ruby's mum and there was nothing that I would have changed. Ruby continued to develop and she reached all her milestones: sitting up, crawling, feeding herself and just trying to be independent. Her favourite foods were Farley's rusk, quavers, wotsits, spaghetti bolognese and yoghurt. Her least favourite food was carrot and she would make this known by closing her tiny mouth. Even at this age, she had her own mind and she was so stubborn. I wonder where she got that from? Being a mum was a blessing and I looked forward to the days ahead.

My World Collapsed

In mid-June of 2007, I noticed Ruby did not seem herself. They say a mother's instinct is always right. I observed her attentively for a while, until she appeared to be herself again. However, towards the end of June I remember being at work and receiving a call from the nursery saying that Ruby had not been well. She had a temperature, so I was asked to collect her. I went to the nursey and picked her up and when I held her, she felt extremely hot. I immediately took her to the doctor who examined her and concluded that it was probably a virus and that I should continue to keep an eye on her and give her calpol on a regular basis. I vividly remember covering her in prayers and this seemed to work. A week or two went by. She seemed fine; she liked playing with her sister and they created an inseparable bond.

Saturday 8th July 2007

Saturday 8th July 2007. This is a day I will never forget. As a family, we continued with life and routines and we were doing our normal chores. I had given Ruby some lunch but after a while, she started vomiting. I was scared as I did not know what was wrong with her. I had never seen someone vomit that much. I decided to take her straight to the hospital. I drove whilst Ruby's dad held her and her sister came with us. On the way to the hospital, Ruby continued to vomit and she was constantly crying.

HOPE

We went straight to Heartlands Accident and Emergency. I explained Ruby's symptoms over the last few weeks and after a while they wanted to do some tests, to determine exactly was wrong with her. They did a Lumbar puncture, which involved her having a needle put in her spine to collect blood for testing.

I could not watch her have this and told her dad to go in with her. I just kept crying, as I knew in my gut that something was wrong. I wanted to swap places with my darling Ruby, as she was only seven months old. I could bear the pain. She was far too young to be going through this type of illness. Ruby and her dad returned, he said she was fine and that all the doctors and nurses loved her.

I phoned my mum and dad and the rest of the family to let them know what had happened; they said they would be supporting us in prayer. In fact, mum and dad came to the hospital; I was so grateful for this, as I needed parents by my side. A little while after they had left, Ruby's dad and my stepdaughter also left, as it was getting late. The hospital staff member confirmed that Ruby would have to stay in overnight and my heart sank to the floor, I thought, 'My little girl is so unwell, they will not let her out'. Naturally, I stayed with my little gem! I asked her dad to get us both some clothing and personal items and I remember throughout the night I just kept holding her, praying and singing encouraging songs.

Sunday 9th July 2007

I remember it was around 12.30 a.m. and I felt tired from the night before, being Ruby's 'watchman'. I would never imagine what was to happen next and to this day, it still brings tears to my eyes; our world was about to change and there was nothing I could do about it, I was powerless. A Doctor in a white coat came into our room with a nurse; I was not asleep, my mind was wide awake and racing, wondering what was wrong with my daughter. The doctor confirmed that they had received the results from the blood test. My heart was beating so fast, that I felt a little dizzy. I could sense it was not good news, the look on their faces gave it away. They asked where Ruby's dad was, I felt cold as I prepared to brace myself. He was coming back so they said if I wished, they could wait till he returns before stating their diagnosis. "Are they crazy"? I thought to myself. "No", I blurted out. I needed to know immediately, I was sick with worry. I knew I would not be able to rest or think about anything else until I could find out what was happening with my daughter. I remember hearing the word leukaemia and the rest became a big blur. I burst out crying, I could not stop the floods of tears streaming down my face. "We are 99.9% sure your daughter Ruby has this", they stated. I froze as they proceeded to tell me that this diagnosis was my little Ruby's death sentence. I sat there in absolute horror and could not figure out what to do next.

Death; that's what we think when we hear of people being diagnosed with leukaemia or cancer. Whether they are young or old. My mind was numb, I could not think straight. They explained the next step was Ruby's transferral to Birmingham Children's hospital, to begin treatment straight away. 'Wow', I thought, this was very serious and was far too much to deal with. How could my little gem have gone from possibly having a virus, to having a life-threatening illness, in such a short space of time; I was bewildered. This felt so surreal, I was all alone and I felt so isolated. Even though the darkest moment in my life, I knew my God was with me every step of the way. It was just a feeling I had of His omnipotent presence, being all-knowing.

I dreaded the fact that I would need to figure out how to tell my family. The nurse in the room encouraged me to trust God. When they left the room, I immediately picked up my mobile and phoned Ruby's dad; he could sense in my voice the severity of the news. I said I would tell him when he returns to the hospital but just like me, he was adamant to be told, there and then. When he heard, I knew he was in a state of shock. When he arrived, we just hugged and cried, with our precious gem in the middle of us. We also prayed because at this point there was no one else we could turn to but God almighty. After he had gone, it was just me and Ruby. I did not sleep. I thought about the extensive treatment of chemotherapy and what her body would have to go through. She would have hair loss. She had beautiful hairstyles done by me, I was so proud. She had lovely thick, long hair but she was going to lose this. I did not know of any other treatment that made you worse before you got better. It was around 7.00 a.m., I thought I needed to inform the family, my parents and my sisters, before they went to church, so I could ask them to say a special prayer. Before I could even say the word Leukaemia, they knew it was serious as I was just crying when I tried to tell them. All were in shock, yet they gave so much encouragement with regard to trusting God and keeping our faith.

I believed that Ruby's ill-health was a test which would ultimately make the family unit stronger. We managed to get through the morning. Ruby's Dad and my stepdaughter returned and later that afternoon, Ruby was transferred to the children's hospital, accompanied by her dad. I drove my car with my stepdaughter and my thoughts whirling around in my head. My mind was restless, trying to comprehend how this was fact and what was fiction. Was this a bad dream, that I will never wake up from? I assured myself that when I do wake up, everything will be fine. Surely, this is a mistake?

When we arrived on the cancer ward, I was in total disbelief, seeing children of various ages and nationalities with drips, loss of hair. I could not hold back the tears, as they fell to my cheeks. It was there and then that I decided that I needed to be with my darling daughter, for as long as she needed me. Work would be the last thing on my mind as I would be taking time off. This was another chapter of our lives, in which only the grace and mercy of God could help us through.

Reality Used to be a Friend of Mine

I remember us trying to take in this new hospital environment, one that none of us had been exposed to. My stepdaughter and me were struggling, whilst Ruby's dad tried his best to be strong for us all; however I knew he too was hurting inside. Little Ruby was the apple of his eye. Our Rubees, as young as she was, God allowed her to fight till the end. Any of us would have traded places with her, if we could.

The staff members were kind and began showing us all the facilities on the ward; one parent could stay with their child. I knew it would be me who stayed, that was not up for debate. As a mother, I could not bear to be away from her because as any mother knows, you want your child to be comforted at all times. The staff member explained that as this was the weekend, the ward was not as full as it usually was, as some children had gone home for weekend visits. I pondered solemnly on the fact that I would be seeing even more children without any hair tomorrow. This is just too much and I found it hard to cope. I went to the bathroom and burst into floods of tears. I stayed there for a while, simply crying my eyes out. I even questioned God. Why us? Why our jewel? But it was clear, why not us? Other families had to go through it, we were no different, why wish this on someone else? The fact that we had God with us, would make it much easier to bear. Being in that bathroom was one of those moments, I felt enveloped by fear. Not knowing the outcome was overwhelming and this was where we had to trust God. Even if our faith was as small as a mustard seed, it was all we could hold on to.

I am a strong woman but this time I needed God to carry me through. I contacted my parents asking if they could come up for some moral support; they came and brought some food for us. We tried to eat, but only had small amounts as we could not eat at a time like this. Then it suddenly hit me and I came to realise that this was going to be our new home for a while, so we would have to get used to it instantly and manage, the best way we could. When placed in the unknown, it can become intimidating and unnerving at times; it is like walking on shaky ground and you never know if it will give way under your feet. We often become so complacent in our own familiar surroundings, however God has a sure way of catching your attention when it is time for change.

After praying, the family left; I just wanted to feel safe. The first night in the hospital was daunting, so many different new sounds, systematic bleeps from machines. The dedicated staff members doing their checks on the children whilst administering medication. During the night, there were periods of silence, assuming that most were asleep but not me; oh no I just could not comprehend how we managed to get to this stage. My one and only biological daughter, I still felt in shock. I kept my eyes fixed on Ruby throughout the night. They had to give her fluids via a cannula they had put into her hand from earlier. Ruby cried when they did this and I joined in too. It was unbearable seeing her in so much pain, as I glanced across at her, I noticed her body had started to swell, causing her breathing to become shallow. I informed the nurse, it all became too distressing because I could see she was struggling to breathe. I demanded to speak to a consultant as she was deteriorating, in the end they had to reduce the amount of fluid that was going into her body. Then it dawned on me, I was her mouthpiece and I was going to speak up for her every step of the way, no matter what, as she was not able to do this for herself.

Over the next few days, various tests were carried out. They confirmed that Ruby had stage three acute myeloid leukaemia (AML), which is cancer of the blood. In children, this was one of the worst types of cancers. They talked us through her treatment, which would involve four blocks of chemotherapy, each block lasting around four weeks, with a week-long home visit between each. It was evident that testing times were ahead of us all and I felt daunted by the process. I wanted to swap places with her so bad. Especially when they went through possible side effects; hair loss, mouth sores, loss of

HOPE

appetite, nausea, vomiting, diarrhoea, fatigue, increased risk of infections, easy bruising, bleeding, low blood cell counts (red blood cells, platelets, white blood cells) and possibly not being able to have children when she was older.

The tears kept coming. 'Why, Why, Why?', I kept asking. Life seemed so unfair, Ruby was only seven months old and the thought of her little body having to go through this was horrific. However, It had to be done if she was to recover. We tried our very best to be positive and reminded ourselves on a daily basis that with God, all things are possible. The next day, Ruby was scheduled to have a procedure, which involved having a central line put into a vein in her chest, so that the chemotherapy drug could be administered. She was promptly moved to a side room on the High Dependency Unit (HDU). I was glad because it enabled us to have privacy with en-suite facilities and a telephone. We tried to make it as homely as we could, by ensuring Ruby had some of her favourite toys. One of her favourite DVDs was Kirk Franklin; she loved the song 'Hosanna', which she woke up to each morning, dancing and clapping. To this day, I still find it hard to listen to that song, as it reminds me of my gem.

I remember thanking God for comforting us through all of this. I had my bible with me and Psalm 91 and Psalm 23 were becoming my favourite scriptures and Ruby's too. When I read the bible to her, she always tried to grab

HOPE

it from me, leaving me with some torn pages. I still have this bible and every so often I look at it and smile. "Yes, Jesus loves me this I know, for the bible tells me so", I sang this to Ruby every night.

I knew family, friends and the church were all praying. The support we had was overwhelming, the phone calls, the texts and the 'get well soon' cards. The love even stretched from overseas, which demonstrated everyone's love and concern. It was tough, as we had to restrict visits to immediate family only, due to risks of infection, due to Ruby's immune system being so low. We could not take any risks. However, there was one person who got away with visiting Ruby; my dear friend, Pauline. Being a community matron, we allowed her, as when she visited she would ensure the nurses and doctors were taking good care of Ruby and if something was not right, she would inform them. They had to get it right, no matter what.

The day came for Ruby to have her central line put in. I remember her dad, my mum and me were in the room and we prayed before she was taken down to the theatre. We walked down with her and watched the staff member give her the anaesthetic, then we had to leave. The staff member reassured us that our daughter would be fine. I remember returning to the lift and feeling so overcome with emotion that my knees buckled and I nearly collapsed. Ruby's dad held me, encouraging me that as parents, we must stay strong. Yes, it is hard but we had to trust in God. I tried my best. My mum and I went for lunch to pass the time. It was good to experience normal environments. When we returned, my Uncle Othniel and Auntie Dell came to visit and to see how we were doing; they said they would wait with us.

It wasn't long before the staff member said we could go down to the recovery room to collect Ruby. All had gone well. We greeted her with the biggest smiles, she too was happy to see us. Two small plastic green tubes in her hands caught my attention; she refused to let go of them. I asked the staff member what they were and they started to laugh and stated they were mouth pieces, used in the theatre. When Ruby woke up, she got hold of them and would not let go, so they said she could keep them. We were all laughing, Rubees was so funny. We then returned to the ward, where my uncle and auntie were waiting to see Ruby. When they saw her, I could see their faces, a sad and concerned look came across their eyes. As she was slightly swollen, her central line was visible as was the cannula in her hand. As my uncle held her, she began to cry; he became upset, as it was clear she was in pain. After words of encouragement and support were given, they both left. I am so thankful and grateful for all they have done and continue to do.

It was time for Ruby to begin the first block of treatment and the nurses came around her bed. They wore aprons, goggles and long gloves covering their arms. I could not help but think, 'these chemotherapy drugs must be so powerful, what would they be doing to the inside of my baby?'. I was concerned but we had no choice, we had to trust God. The drugs were administered and I watched Ruby like a hawk, looking out for any side effects. To be honest, I was more intimidated by it all. Ruby, despite it all, always had a smile on her face. Her strength was inspiring. After days being on the ward, we developed friendships with other parents, who were also going through the same misfortune as us. One couple had a daughter who was a month younger than Ruby and was diagnosed with Acute Lymphoblastic leukaemia (ALL), a form cancer of the white blood cells. Who knew there were so many different types? Over the weeks, we became very good friends, especially as mothers, we spent most days together, caring for our children. Our daughters became the best of friends and when their health permitted them, they played together and shared their toys with each other. I was happy to see Ruby having a friend to play with, someone who was of similar age but as parents, we discussed how we wished our children's friendship was under different circumstances. However, as difficult as it was, we learned to value and appreciate what we had.

On the ward, we were all different; a collection of nationalities and cultures. We all had one thing in common; our children were diagnosed with a life-threatening illness. Naturally, we were terrified however, we had each other. Every week, there were new children being admitted onto the ward, along with that look of distress from the new parents.

This is the reason I wrote this book, to help other parents deal with losing their child. After I had settled on the ward, I also helped other parents settle in, showing them all the facilities on the ward, especially the parents' room. I was able to be a friend and a support mechanism for some, giving words of encouragement and prayer. "How do you do it? How can you be so positive when your daughter is here and being treated for Leukaemia?", I would often be asked.

My response would always be consistent, "I have hope in God; it's my faith right now that keeps me going and enables me to encourage others in such sad times. I believe in God and know that He will take care of my problems. He is truly with us in every situation!"

18th July 2007 and my sister, Sharmaine, who was expecting, had gone into labour. I remember her ringing me early in the morning to say her waters had broken. I wished her well and said to phone me once she had the baby. That day I was on tender hooks, waiting for any news. Later on, she called telling me she had a baby girl and named her Kiarah. I remember leaving Ruby with the nurses, to go to City Hospital to see my niece. When I got there and saw my sister, I joked and said that Kiarah could not wait to come out. She could see Ruby was getting all the attention and wanted some of it too. Thank God both mother and baby were doing well. I felt empathy for my family, as over the next few days they had two hospitals to visit. However, they were supportive as always and I felt so grateful.

Ruby sailed through the first block of treatment, with side effects of vomiting and diarrhoea. However, a week or so later, I noticed something. The first time it happened, I had just given her a bath and washed her hair. I looked down and saw quite a lot of her hair in the water. The tears just started falling down my face. Her beautiful hair; I questioned why this had to happen to my baby girl. Why did it have to be Ruby who got sick? I had to quickly come to terms with what was happening and as hard as it was, I had to cope the best way that I could. I was at the hospital for three weeks before I finally went home. It wasn't that family or friends did not offer to stay overnight with Ruby but I knew I could not have left her any earlier. I needed to be there throughout all this madness. No one could take my place of being her mother and this was *my* fight as a mother. This was my journey, no matter how difficult it was. Despite all of this heartache, I still had to liaise with my manager at work, sending in sick notes and I had my union representative visiting me at the hospital, just to check how I was doing. He showed empathy and concern for us as a family and for the other parents and children on the ward; he could see how devastating it was for us all. I could see his eyes welling up but I assured him that I was fine, as my faith was keeping me going. Nonetheless, having a sick child is an unsettling feeling.

Whilst being a mother to Ruby, there were many other roles I had to try hard to maintain and juggle at the same time. I was also a mother to my stepdaughter but I felt that she was being neglected. All the attention was on her younger sister, so I had to ensure that we had quality time together when we could. It was also important that her schoolwork did not suffer. Sometimes, she did her homework at the hospital, as she wanted to spend time with her baby sister. As a family, we had to stay united. I remember cooking family meals at the hospital, just so we could properly spend time together. I was also trying to be a wife. I had many pressures and I know it was not by my own strength that I was able to cope with everything but the strength of God, holding my hand through this process. He placed people in my life at the time, like Sister Daley who would phone me every day and encourage me with the word of God. Thank you so much for the love.

Taking Ruby home

The day came for Ruby to have a week at home; we were so ecstatic, this day could not have come quick enough. After ensuring that her blood count and platelet levels were fine, we were able to go home. We had so many things we were eagerly anticipating, while also enjoying a bit of normality. For me personally, I was looking forward to not having to hear bleeps during the night, having some privacy, not having to sleep on fold up beds, being able to cook home-cooked foods and for us to be a normal family again. On leaving the ward, we said goodbye to our friends; how I wished that we did not have to come back but the date and time we were given to return to the ward said otherwise.

We arrived at our terrestrial haven and walking into the house was just a wonderful experience. The familiar surroundings were so comforting; all we could do was thank God for all He had done, to get us this far. For a few days, we managed a routine and did normal things. However, Ruby started to become unwell; she had a temperature and was vomiting. We took her to heartlands hospital and on arrival I informed them of her symptoms and that we were on a break at home for the week. They monitored her and whilst she was there, Ruby was still vomiting, so they decided that they needed to do some tests in order to identify the problem. All the while, she was constantly crying and appeared to be in some pain. I let her dad go with her, as I knew I would not able to bear to see the injections. My stepdaughter and I stayed in the cubicle. We decided to pray and read the scriptures, Psalm 23 and Psalm 91. It was all we could do, to pray. After what felt like eternity, Ruby returned. When we saw her, we laughed and began to praise God;

HOPE

we did not care who was watching because what we witnessed was nothing short of a miracle, as Ruby was sitting up on the bed, clapping her hands and singing. Even the staff members were in shock; they could not believe the transformation. I shared that we trust in God and He did not fail us. They confirmed Ruby was suffering from constipation, hence the pain. They decided to keep Ruby in overnight and give her medication to relieve the problem. Thankfully the next day, Ruby was discharged home. It was good to be back just enjoying normality, whatever that was now. Over the next few days, we enjoyed having our daughter back at home. Apart from immediate family, we did not allow any other visitors.

We had phone calls from some requesting to visit but we had to be firm and decline. We had no choice as Ruby's immune system was so low. We were coming to the end of the week of being at home and I was getting everything together. I remember at one point, I just sat on the bed and I could feel the tears coming down; this was a fantasy, more like a holiday. Just the thought of our jewel having to return to the hospital, was heart breaking. Ruby was going to start the 2nd block of treatment, which was much more 'intense' and the side effects would be worse. God, how we need you right now, by ourselves we cannot make it, this journey is too hard. We pray for strength, so we can make it to the end.

That night, I made Ruby her favourite meal, spaghetti bolognese and we played with her. She also enjoyed playing with her toys and just being the centre of attention; this was her moment. I don't think any of us slept much that night. We had to be on the ward for 9.00 a.m. Driving to the hospital I felt nausea, if I could have turned the car back, I would have done so. Right then, it was like I needed to have some reassurance; all I heard so strongly was "go in my name, I am with you always and I will be with you till the very end". I knew it was God's inner voice ushering me on. When you go through crisis, you get real spiritual.

We arrived on the ward to see some familiar faces, and some not so familiar. There were new children on the ward; their parents will be going through what we went through initially. Everyone was glad to see Ruby; she had developed her own fan club, among other children, their relatives and the staff members. They all wanted to see her, of course she was a child of the King and she gave others so much hope. This journey taught me that our tests are a testimony to others. Through it we can encourage others to trust God, no matter what the situation may look like because in God there is hope, strength and peace. Even if it feels like your whole world is falling apart, God will not let you down. When you feel like you cannot take another step, be assured that He is carrying you forward.

HOPE

How we managed to function on a day-to-day basis, was nothing short of a miracle. God was carrying us through the terrain. After settling on the ward, the Consultant came to see us as a family and explained about the next block of treatment and side effects. Ruby had to have eye drops instilled every four hours. Heart and kidney scans were required, to make sure there was no damage from the chemotherapy. This felt so surreal, however as a family, we got on with it. We had our up and down days but after all, we're only human. After many days of having treatment, I noticed Ruby was not eating much, she just closed her mouth to most foods. This became a concern for the staff members, as Ruby was losing weight rapidly. I was also so concerned. No matter how anyone tried to feed her, she would not take it but she did have her Farley's rusk, quavers, wotsits and yoghurts. I think her mouth was becoming too sore because of the chemotherapy. They treated her for it, but even when it did get better, our dear Ruby refused to eat, probably out of fear of reliving the pain. This resulted in a staff member asking the chef from the restaurant at the hospital to speak to me about Ruby's favourite foods at home, the ingredients I used and how I prepared them. I told him Ruby loves spaghetti bolognese, steak and kidney pie, pasta, rice and custard. The chef tried to prepare some of these meals the way I did them at home. Some of the other parents could not believe it when the meals came up in a trolley onto the ward and Ruby's meals always came up differently, on a different plate, wrapped with her name on. "How did you manage that?", they enquired. I thought to myself, 'It's not what you know, it's who you know and I know the name Jesus.' I just said she is special and she really was that and such an amazing human being. I personally think that she was making a point, just like her mother. She was a fussy eater; if the food did not taste quite right, she was not going to eat it no matter how hard you tried to encourage her. That's my girl!

Ruby continued with her treatment and she had her good and bad days. At times, she was in pure pain, which saddened me deeply. No one would wish for their child to experience any form of pain. If only I could have changed places with her. Her dad and sister felt exactly the same. In fact, all the family felt the same.

Our dearest Ruby, this was her fight and hers only; our God was with her every step of the way. Throughout, Ruby's white blood cells, red blood cells and platelet counts were checked. There were a few times that she required blood and platelet transfusions because of her low counts. It was then I realised that within our ethnic group, more donors were required to come forward. I recognised the importance of this at one of the saddest times of my life. We learnt so much whilst being in hospital, especially with the different types of cancers and leukaemia. I really did not know there was so many, for example, Wilm's tumour, Neuroblastoma, Ewing Sarcoma and Hodgkin lymphoma, just to name a few. We really got to know some of the children on the ward and they all had a special place in my heart. I remember one parent asking me to pray for her child, as the consultant informed her that her son had further tumours on his lungs and there is nothing more that they can do. When she told me, my eyes welled up, but I had to be strong, and I prayed but sadly the teenager lost his fight.

Whilst in the hospital, we met with Macmillan nurses and they helped us in applying for benefits, such as disability allowance for Ruby. They would ensure that we had everything we needed whilst at hospital and when we went home. Sadly, we could not apply to the 'Make a Wish Foundation', who helped children with life-threatening illnesses, as Ruby was too young. So many of the children were given the opportunity to travel and do amazing things, such as a fun trip to Disneyland. Seeing the smile on their faces was so inspiring. So much joy, knowing that despite all that they were going through, the children were doing their best to enjoy life. As we approached the end of the second block of treatment, thank God, Ruby appeared to sail through it, what a relief. She showed pure determination and grit, no matter what the doctors and nurses said, she showed strength. Although she was going through treatment, she also reached her milestones. She began to walk at nine months. We returned home after the end of treatment and we said our goodbyes to the staff. I did not want to ever go back.

During her second block of treatment, I started to go home on Thursday and Saturday; I felt confident in leaving Ruby, as her dad stayed with her. I know it was God's strength that kept me during these times, because I still managed to go to church on a Sunday morning, leading people into worship, despite all that I was going through at the time and it gave me a glimmer of hope. I had to do this to let others who were possibly struggling, know that you can praise God through your difficult times if you ask Him to help you. That's what I did, praised God; the way may have looked dark, I did not know what the outcome of the journey was going to be but I had faith and trusted Him.

Since Ruby had done quite well during her second block of treatment, her Consultant said we could have two weeks at home. The look of relief on our faces said it all. THANK YOU, GOD. We had so much fun spoiling her; we even took her out a couple of times, once to Cannon Hill Park, which she thoroughly enjoyed and we also took her to church. Everyone was glad to see our perfect gem, although we had to be strict and did not allow anyone to pick her up, we just could not take any form of risk. It was hard to do that but we had no choice, we had to be wise.

Finally, we felt like a normal family, just being able to do normal things again. However, I remember bathing Ruby

HOPE

one day and I noticed her central line was loose, like it was coming out. Instinctively I felt she was trying to tell me something. No more treatment? Immediately, I phoned the hospital and they arranged for the Macmillan nurse to visit. We were praying as the thought of having to return to hospital was not what we wanted. By the time the nurse arrived, the central line had totally come out, I looked at Ruby to see if she was in any pain, she did not appear to be, in fact, she was being her usual jolly self. All the nurse did was put a dressing on the wound and said she did not have to go to hospital as there was no bleeding. We thanked God; we just thought Ruby was just so funny, nothing phased her. A few days later, we returned to hospital for Ruby to have a new central line put back in and commence her third block of treatment, our baby Ruby's petite body has been through so much, yet she kept fighting. One more block of treatment to go, then we're done. We can get back to normality. We don't know the plan of God but we knew His words: *Jeremiah 29:11: NIV: "For I know the plans I have for you," declares the Lord, "plans to prosper you and not to harm you, plans to give you hope and a future."*

Despite all, Ruby continued to make us laugh, in particular when the nurses came to look after her, she made it very clear if she did not like a nurse, by making grunting noises if they had to pick her up. Or she would try to wriggle free out of their arms. It was even funnier when watching some of the nurses trying to gain Ruby's love, she never budged. She was hilariously stubborn; her facial expressions said it all, she got that from me. For those nurses she liked, she was a little ANGEL and co-operated with them effortlessly. Ruby was just being Ruby and she would not change for anyone. I later learnt that all the nurses wanted to look after her; some wanted to take her home. As one nurse said, it was worth coming to work just to see Ruby's smile. I was so honoured to know that our rare gem, a precious individual, was so popular; they called her a shining star on the ward. Ruby continued through the third block of treatment; a couple of times she appeared to have caught an infection, having constant diarrhoea and eventually she had to be isolated. I did not mind, as we had our own room. On most occasions, we used to play gospel DVDs and CDs, which just encouraged us to continue to hold onto God, no matter what, in sickness and in health. Despite all, God deserves our praises. I remember one day sitting in the room and watching a new Kirk Franklin DVD I had brought the day before. A nurse came into the room, to make Ruby's bed, turning to me she said, "You've changed the DVD, is it new?" I said, "Yes, how did you know?" The nurse replied, "I really like to listen to the songs in this room, they make the ward feel peaceful. In fact, all the staff members want to come into this room because of the music and the sense of hope it gives us". I realised that every trial or tribulation we encounter in life is a testimony for others. God places us in environments that we would never envisage ourselves to be in but it's not about us, it's about God.

Eventually, Ruby's infection had gone and we moved back into the main bay, Amen. As much as I missed the privacy of being in a room, it was nice to be back in the bay, as there was so much more going on, more people to speak to. Ruby had come to the end of her third block of treatment. What a fighter. A daughter who showed nothing but amazing strength. Going home in October 2007, I thought about how Ruby would be one-year-old on 19th November 2007. Would we reach this special date? I had faith. How would we celebrate this special day?

I discussed it with Ruby's dad and sister; we wanted to have a party for her but knew she would be in hospital having her last block of treatment. The week at home went by so fast, we did Ruby's favourite things: helping her to play with her toys, playing with her sister, playing with her dad; he would do anything for her. Family members always came around, as long as they were well, which Ruby enjoyed as she was so close to them. If she was crying, all would rush to comfort her, she was spoilt for choice and we would not have had it any other way.

During my time at the hospital, I witnessed at least two children who sadly passed away and I did not want that future for my little fighting angel. I witnessed the pain of the parents' worlds collapsing. How does a parent bury

HOPE

their child? It is not right I tell you, brothers and sisters. I did not realise that months down the line, I too would have to go through this very traumatic experience myself and bear the unimaginable pain, of feeling a loss, followed by not wanting to live but die.

The Final Block

My mind was restless the night before returning to the hospital for Ruby's final block of treatment. God had been so good to us as a family; this journey had not been easy for any of us, however He had kept His guiding hand on us so far and we were on the last leg of this journey. Thank goodness. This endeavour brought some new experiences; pain, much heartache and joy. We had met so many extraordinary people who have impacted our lives. I did not like what I had to go through but it has made me the person I am today.

I remember us praying as a family that night, thanking God for all He had done. The day came for us to return, and as always, we had to be on the ward for 9.00 a.m. This time, there was a different feeling for me, I think for us all because we knew this was Ruby's final block of treatment. This time seemed so far away from when she started her initial treatment. Everyone was so glad to see her and complimented how well she looked, our jewel looked so beautiful, despite all the treatment she was undertaking. She had so many different coloured hats after her hair loss, which matched her clothes and I always ensured she was colour co-ordinated from head to toe, whilst she was in hospital. I started a trend on the ward, some parents did not bother to dress their child in their day clothes, they used to wear the hospital gowns but once they saw Ruby being dressed the way she was, they also followed. Again our angel set a trend and this is how God can use a bad situation to work wonders in our lives. As I said earlier, she was SPECIAL and an EXCEPTIONAL child.

Whilst Ruby commenced her final treatment, we were preparing to organise her first birthday party. The staff members kindly agreed that it could be held on the ward. We had decorations, food, presents for all the children attending the party, as well as Ruby's presents of course. We bought our little Ruby Wax a walker for her first birthday and a very special cake with the word 'Princess' on it because that's what she was, OUR DARLING PRINCESS. This last block of treatment appeared to be taking its toll on her little body and Ruby had her good and bad days. She appeared to be in some pain and at times did not liked to be touched, even by me her mother. On several occasions, morphine had to be administered, which eased the pain and she then became her usual, lively self. When she was in pain, the tears would fall and I wished I could take her pain away and somehow absorb it all for her. I was reminded, 'Maxine, this is not your fight but Ruby's fight and with God, she will fight till the end.'

The day came for Ruby to have her first birthday party and we had to bring everything to the hospital. I remember going into town the week before, to get an outfit for her. After looking in several shops, I went into H&M's and saw a gold dress, with an oriental looking pattern on it. The dress came with a head band, but Ruby had hair loss, so how would the band look? I knew she would look so adorable in it, so I purchased it straight away. When we dressed Ruby on the day, we could not believe how beautiful and gorgeous she looked. Her dad incessantly took pictures whilst we admired her. Everyone commented on how flawless she looked. It was an honour to be chosen by God to be Ruby's mum. It was priceless. Nothing could take that feeling away. I do however wish that my motherhood experience was much longer than the brief encounter I had. The staff members on the ward were fantastic in providing us with everything that we needed; it was lovely to see all the family and a few close friends we had invited. Everyone joined in, children who could attend and their parents.

Ruby did enjoy herself the best way she could, although I could see she was in some pain, she brightened up throughout the day. The staff members commended us as a family, for the way we organised the party and how we got everyone on the ward together the way we did; they had never seen that happen before. Again, I was reminded that our tests are not for ourselves or just for our families but for touching the lives of others. After the party had ended and everyone had gone home, I studied her presents; she received so much, there were so many colourful packages.

HOPE

I started to meticulously count down the days for when Ruby would be able to return home and for us spending quality time as a family. Christmas and New Year; the possibilities overwhelmed me. Finally, the day arrived, 27th November 2007 and we were so excited. There were so many goodbyes and gift items to give to the staff members. The thought of never having to go back again soothed me. Many staff members, children and their parents, became emotional when it was time for us to leave. For most, Ruby was the life and soul of the ward. She brought so much joy, everyone was just drawn to her, she had left an indelible mark on the ward; she was definitely unique in her own right.

We ensured that we had all of Ruby's medication, all the necessary contact details for all the professionals who had been involved in her care and all follow-up appointments were given. We gave out 'thank-you' cards and presents to the staff members on the ward. This didn't feel sufficient for all the hard work they had done as their dedication and their commitment was impeccable.

As we left, I cried; I was grateful to God for all that He had done. I remember us leaving the hospital as a family, walking down the corridor. I felt free, it was like a weight lifted off me. We could not get home quick enough, as we entered onto the drive and into the house, we brought Ruby inside, I had managed to come home prior

HOPE

to tidy up and do some grocery shopping, ensuring we had all essentials because I just wanted to spend the next few days at home, not going anywhere, chilling, relaxing and making the most of this special milestone. We settled at home, we had so much to give God thanks for, He delivered us from a dark valley. Just being able to enjoy our own surroundings was a privilege. As a family, we got back into a routine. Ruby's sister would go to school, when she returned home, Ruby would stretch out her hands to be picked up by her and the laughing would start; it was like they had special secrets together. Ruby's dad continued to work as an interpreter and I stayed at home, as my priority was being with my gem. How I loved spending time with Ruby Wax (as her sister named her), being at home with her was like heaven, a real dream come true.

I did not think about returning to work, all I wanted to do was to be with Ruby. I continued to report to work periodically. We were able to take Ruby to church, she loved dancing and clapping her hands to the music. Everyone was overjoyed to see her and commented on how well she looked. She did look beautiful, especially with her colour co-ordinated hats matching her outfits. (She was gorgeous). We thanked God in the midst of our storms, He had brought us so far as a family. It was coming up to Christmas, I knew it was going to be fantastic, Ruby would be spoilt rotten and why not? She deserved it. Days prior to Christmas, Ruby had a follow-up appointment at the children's hospital. I was not worried as she appeared well and I remember dressing her in a brown top, jeans, hat and a three-quarter length coat, she looked stunning as per normal.

When we arrived at the outpatient department, everyone was in awe of her, which made me smile. It was good to see familiar faces. We caught up on what had been happening in our lives but it was so sad when we learnt that during the weeks of being at home, a few of the children we knew had lost their lives. The pain I felt, I just held onto my Ruby tighter; I did not want to imagine the pain their parents must have gone through.

Eventually, Ruby's Dad and I went to see the consultant; when he saw Ruby, he commented on how well she looked and that she was a walking miracle. He confirmed to our delight, that Ruby was in remission and we should go home and have a wonderful Christmas and he would see Ruby in six months' time. We couldn't keep the smiles from our faces. We could not contain ourselves; what a relief, the storm is over. When we left, we were so elated, we had to give God thanks and praise. We decided to visit the staff and children on ward 15, as we had some cards and presents for the staff members. When we got onto the ward, everyone was so glad to see us and commented on how healthy Ruby looked. We also shared the news with the staff members about Ruby being in remission and they all were pleased for us. We again thanked the team on the ward for all they had done, we were so grateful. We left the hospital thinking never to return ever again. However, we were not to know the journey that was ahead of us. On returning home, we contacted all the family and close friends, sharing our fantastic news. Now we could think about Christmas, buying presents for both our girls and families. Knowing that this would be a special Christmas, we would go overboard in spoiling Ruby because she had gone through so much during these turbulent five months.

In 2007, Christmas day came, how we all woke up early to open our presents, just to see the smiles on our dear jewel's face was precious. How she got excited opening all her presents, in fact, she had the most. On the day, we visited family members and Ruby was the centre of attention. She had even more presents from grandparents, aunties and uncles and I wondered where we would put them all! Storing presents was a good problem to have, considering everything we had been put though.

Christmas came and then we celebrated New Year; we all went to church on New Year's Eve. It was a time of reflection on the old year. What a test we have had as a family, it made our bond stronger but we thanked God that we had made it so far and were still standing. *"I shall not die, but live and declare the works of the Lord."*

Psalm 118:7. AMEN! This whole experience could have destroyed us as a family but with God's strength and ongoing love we were able to overcome. This was going to be a New Year of new beginnings for everyone. Naively thinking the worst was over, we looked forward to celebrating happy times again. We still enjoyed a few wonderful moments, such as attending my niece's christening on 13th January 2008. Again, as much as it was Kiarah's day, Ruby was also the centre of attention because everyone knew what she had gone through. By this time, I remember that Ruby's hair was starting to grow back, I was so happy to see her silky baby hair growing through, I could not wait till it grew to a length that was long enough to comb, plait and to make pretty intricate styles with bobbles. I had all the styles planned in my head. Sunday 20h January 2008, Ruby and my stepdaughter and I had attended Sunday evening service at church; it was lovely. I had the opportunity to give my testimony and inspire the congregation with hope. I spoke about what the family had gone through and Ruby being in remission, how we just thanked and praised God for the miraculous work He had done. The joy of the night was seeing Ruby dancing and clapping her hands to the choruses that were being sung. It was like she was dancing for dear life, the smile that was on her face and the squeals of joy coming from her were truly heart-warming. Church members turned around to watch her, she was definitely the star of the night.

The Last Lap

On Monday 21st January 2008, I remember waking up and noticing Ruby did not appear to be well, she felt hot to touch and started vomiting. Immediately, my mother's instinct kicked in and thought it best to get her to hospital to be checked out. I kept thinking it will just be a virus, surely, God would not allow us to go through Ruby having leukaemia again. Deep down on the inside of my heart, I knew it was not going to be good news. I braced myself for what was about to happen next.

Even though Heartland's hospital was nearer to us, we decided to take our gem, Ruby, to the children's hospital, as they had her records there and the staff members would be more familiar with her case. Ruby's Dad, her sister and I brought her onto the outpatients' ward. They all appeared shocked to see us. I explained all her symptoms and it was decided that Ruby would have to stay in to have tests to determine what was wrong. To be honest, I could sense the bad news. I did not need test results to tell me that the leukaemia had returned; I thought she would fight just as she did before and she would be fine. Ruby underwent some tests and that familiar feeling of worry, once again greeted us. The staff members said they would have to admit Ruby onto a ward but the ward where she was on before was full, so we had to go to a different one. It was bad enough that

HOPE

we had to return to the hospital, however going onto a different ward made it much more intimidating.

There was nothing we could do but to surrender and trust God. Finally they get us on a ward, I felt out of my comfort zone big time; we did not know anyone, I thought, 'I just want to go home and take Ruby with me.' I didn't want to go through this again; the tears caressed my face. Why? Why? Why God are we going through this again? Had we not gone through enough as a family? I phoned the rest of the family and with a heavy heart informed them of what had happened, they too were in shock to know what had occurred but encouraged us to hold onto faith in God. At this point, it was easier said than done but I knew they were right. For the next few days, various tests were carried out.

Family and very close friends came to visit and we were grateful for their continued support. I remember one visit, from my friend, Pauline. She came on the ward in the room that we were in; she was not impressed with the standard of cleanliness at all and informed the staff members. I had already done so prior but whilst she was there, they gave our room a thorough clean. I also recall that apart from us as parents, she was the last person to see Ruby walking with her walker on that day, as Ruby and I walked with her when she was leaving. Due to the intense treatment, sadly Ruby never had the strength to walk again after that day.

Thank God, not too long after they were able to move us back on ward 15, into a side room. I did not think anything of it but was glad to be back in familiar surroundings. Staff members that we knew, parents and children also; there were some new faces and again, my heart went out to those parents who were new to this journey, as it was not an easy road to travel. The nurses said the consultant would be with us shortly to go through the results of the tests that were carried out. My mind became restless and anxious. Nausea overcame me and I felt physically weak.

The consultant came in and asked us how we were and I said I was scared because as a mother I knew Ruby was unwell. The consultant stated, "The leukaemia has returned with a vengeance and Ruby will need to have another course of chemotherapy but we have not decided on the exact treatment and are considering this." Bang, my worst fears were confirmed. We all looked at each other with the feeling of dread. I could not comprehend it and it was even more baffling, the second time around.

I immediately just hugged and kissed my daughter, reassuring her she would be fine. We would get through this, just as we did before. At times, life can be so cruel but God is faithful till the end. Again, we phoned family members and close friends, informing them of the diagnosis. They all gave us words of encouragement, scriptures and prayers. We tried our best to think that everything would be alright, this was just a setback and we can get through it with God beside us. I was grateful that we had a side room because this time around I really did not want to speak to anyone; I just wanted us to have time to ourselves to take in the new situation. "The leukaemia has come back with vengeance," echoed in my mind, making me worry. Vengeance, why use such a strong word? My immediate thought was of our beautiful girl! She must be in so much pain. I just prayed for God to be with her because no matter what, as parents, there was only so much we could do. The only thing we knew was to continue to trust God, He has brought us this far as a family, surely, He would not leave us now? I had to try to be positive, no matter what the results. I kept thinking Ruby would be fine, all she needed was to have a different course of chemotherapy and she would be fine. The leukaemia would go in the name of Jesus. Never to return again!

In the midst of all of this, our gem, Ruby was being her usual self, although she was in pain, she still had a smile and she continued to be the most popular child on the ward. Although we were hidden away in a side room, everyone wanted to see her. She continued to have favourite staff members, her facial expressions said it all if they were not her favourite. She made us laugh as a family, she was just so comical and her strength was so amazing. In time, Ruby began a different course of treatment and we were hopeful as a family, that this would work.

HOPE in God was all that we had. Again, I stayed with her majority of the time, only going home on Thursday and Saturday evenings, whilst her dad stayed with her. Even during these difficult times again, I continued to go to church each Sunday. Despite all that we were going through, I had to give God thanks and praise. I learned that it was easy to praise God when things were going well but when not so well, it was hard. This was one of those times and it was not by my own strength but through God. Our gem continued to fight with all that she had, never giving up or being defeated.

"I will bless the Lord at all times; His praise shall continually be in my Mouth." **Psalm 34:1** Sometimes whilst being at Church, I thought I was mad. How could I be here whilst my daughter is in hospital suffering with a life-threatening illness? I felt guilty at times but I knew I just had to be there because all I could do was pray for strength to cope with everything that we were going through at the time. Whilst in hospital over the next month, I kept a close eye my little Ruby. Various tests were carried out and there were even talks of a possible bone marrow transplant. Even looking at family members being a possible match gave us hope, as it meant that other options were being discussed.

HOPE

"We could not give up now, we had come too far, no one told us that this road would be easy." We had to fight this mammoth battle of war, knowing that God will deliver us. Days and weeks went by and there did not appear to be much change in our gem's condition. In fact, she was not walking anymore and appeared to have a loss of appetite. I kept thinking positively, that this was just a minor setback, Ruby will be fine and when she is, we will be wondering what the fuss was all about.

Saturday 8th March 2008. It was a normal day being in the hospital, some children had gone home for weekend visits. The ward was not as full and buzzing as normal. We continued to be in a side room, which was a safe-haven for us, it was like our own little world, when we needed those private moments, together as family. Ruby's dad and sister were with Ruby and I; we were having some family time but our gem appeared to be unwell, in pain, had a temperature and was vomiting. The nurse looking after Ruby was concerned and asked for the consultant to come and see her. After a while, he did. He turned to us as parents and said that he would "see us in the meeting room in a few minutes." Ruby's dad and I exchanged worried looks. We knew that having meetings in that particular room, meant that good news was rare. What could they possibly say to us that is worse than what we are going through now? I hugged Ruby, I was so scared. Tears were just streaming down my face. 'She has to get better, she just has to', I thought. I trust God that

HOPE

He will do this; I know Jesus. After an hour or so, we went to see the consultant, as he wanted to give an update on Ruby's condition. I remember walking to the room, I could feel my heart beating rapidly and I felt like I was going to pass out. I prayed silently to God.

Please God, let it be good news. Please let it be that she is responding to treatment and we will be able to go home soon. I desperately clung onto hope. We sat down. I just wanted to hear the prognosis, whether good or bad. The consultant explained that Ruby has had a different course of treatment for the last month or so, which they thought would have worked but it has not. I remember some information being given to us but all I could dwell and focus on was the words, "She has two days to two weeks to live, at the most and there is nothing more we can do for her." I collapsed on the floor and let out a poignant scream. "No, you've got it wrong!!!", I yelled at the top of my lungs. Ruby's Dad's face was soaked in tears. I ran out of the room and off the ward, along the corridor and out to the main entrance. It became hard to breathe. I could not comprehend what we were just told. Not my baby. No way is she going to die, not on my watch. This was a mistake. They've got it all wrong.

They must have? There is no way God would allow my only biological child to die. Life could never be that cruel. I wanted to die myself, right there on the spot. I even thought about walking into the road, so I could be hit by

HOPE

a car. If my gem, Ruby, was going to die, why would I want to live? After what felt like hours, I eventually phoned my parents. I was just crying and crying. I could hardly say the words and I did not want to tell them what I had just been told, they so much adore their Granddaughter but as always, they encouraged me to hold onto God. I am so grateful to them for all that they continue to do. They told me they were coming to see us. I also phoned my sisters and informed them of the devastating news, they too were in disbelief and gave me words of encouragement that no matter what, I could not give up now. I then phoned Pauline, I was just crying and crying, the pain was so unbearable, she too said she would come and see us that day. Eventually, I returned to the ward and went into the room where Ruby was. All I could do was to hold onto her for dear life. Ruby's dad, her sister and I just hugged each other. I felt like this would bring us closer together as a family. That day, other family members came to see us and prayed with us, whilst they also encouraged us with the word of God. It was only prayers that would take us through this time.

My friend, Pauline, came again and visited and also gave us words of encouragement. With everything that had gone on, in the midst of it all, I forgot that our church convention was being held at Bethel Convention Centre the same evening and our church choir would be ministering. So instead of going home, I decided I needed to attend the convention. I already had some clothes at the hospital, so I was able to change there. Pauline said she would stay for a while, also Ruby's dad was staying overnight with her.

Despite the circumstances, I felt I had to go. Before leaving, we all prayed. I kissed my gem and told her that I would see her the next day. I drove to Bethel Convention Centre in West Bromwich, only by God's strength. The feeling of being overwhelmed swept through my soul and drained me; I had so many thoughts whirling around my mind. Would Rubees be okay? It was a terrifying thought to think that the child you gave birth to could be leaving the planet before you. No parent should have to bury their child, it is just not the order of life's cycle. When I got there, I kept looking at everyone, thinking, 'Your lives are so normal'; apart from family members, no one knew what I had gone through today. It was a relief to be in a different environment. I sat, trying to participate and enjoy the service but it was hard. My mind was racing all over the place, I kept thinking of all that had happened earlier. As the choir was due to minister in song, we had to meet together prior, to put on our gowns and pray. As we were in the room, we all had our gowns on but before we began to pray, I said I needed to share my testimony.

I had not planned to do this. With tears spilling down my face, I had to share with them what I had gone through. It had been the most devastating day of my life when the consultant told me that Ruby has two days to two weeks to live, at the most. All I could see were eyes welling up in the room, I continued with sharing the reason I came was to demonstrate that God deserves all of our praises and that we must worship Him in truth and we must sing His praise in good and bad times. We do not go out and minister of our self-seeking selves but seek ye first the Kingdom of God and all His glory. By the time I had finished sharing, I was crying so much but at the same time, I was praising and thanking God for allowing me to encourage others that there is Hope in their own circumstances. I did not know what I was going to face later but I knew that God would be with me. The choir ministered that evening and what a blessing. Weeks later, I was informed by a parent whose child was in the choir, that for them, their favourite part of the convention was my testimony that I had shared with them before ministering, it was so inspiring. They could not believe I was in convention after being told the devastating news. I knew I must be a humbled servant of the Lord our God. I do believe that our difficult times are not only for ourselves but to encourage others. I went home that night feeling more positive than I did earlier that day, despite what was going on. I remember being at home and just looking at some of Ruby's clothes and toys and thinking that she may not wear or play with them again. What would I do? How would I cope? Only with God could we cope.

The next day I went to church, participated in the worship team and I felt uplifted. I went to the hospital, to see my beautiful gem. How could we lose her in this way? We would not. Surely no way would God let this happen? Yes, we have been given this debilitating news but they will see how God works. The following day, the consultant came to us and explained the next steps, either we could take Ruby home and have Macmillan nurses give us support in caring for Ruby, or we could stay at the hospital and let nature take its course, either way it would be to make Ruby as comfortable as possible during her final days. At this point I was thinking, 'They still think she is going to die! Well, that is not our thought'; I made the decision for us all that we would stay in hospital because I felt it was safer.

Although decisions were being made, I knew I was in denial regarding what was happening, it was like my life was playing in slow motion. I thought this was the only way I could cope. We took one day at a time and began to inform more family members and close friends of the prognosis; they were all in state of shock but never stopped encouraging us with the word of God. Special prayers were going up for Ruby, of course, God would answer our prayers. Over the next few days and weeks, we kept watching our gem. She remained with us, I thought to myself, 'She is such a fighter, she is demonstrating that she was not going anywhere, and she was here to stay.' When we got to weeks three and four,

HOPE

I thought definitely they had made a mistake because we were initially told she had two days to two weeks at the most to live and she clearly had surpassed that. Even staff members that had returned from holiday were shocked to see Ruby was still with us. 'Of course, she is she is not going anywhere', I would think. Even family and friends who either visited or called, were in awe as Ruby was still going strong. A small child but what a big fighter she was. 'Don't underestimate the God that we serve.'

It was coming up to my 40th Birthday. The 22nd March. Personally, I could not think about this, how could I with all that was going on? But my family wanted to make a fuss of me, my sisters kindly organised for me to have my nails and my makeup done, I felt spoilt that day, and later in the evening, we went out for a family meal to a Chinese restaurant. I did not want to leave Ruby, as spending every moment with her was precious. Ruby's godmother, Liela, offered to stay with her, whilst we went out. I tried my best to enjoy myself but it was not the same, my mind was just on my little gem; I did phone on several occasions but was reassured that Ruby was fine and not to worry. I was thankful to my family for all they had done in celebrating my milestone birthday, however, it was still a hard day to enjoy without my beautiful gem! Deep on the inside I knew if God brings you to it, He will take you through it.

HOPE

Through it all, I was still having to go through the sickness and policy procedure at work, still sending in sick notes a few times. I even had to go to our head office, which was based in the city centre, attending a scheduled meeting on 16th April 2008. I kept thinking how insensitive they were and I made my feelings known to them but I also knew they had to follow policy and procedure. The outcome of the meeting was that I was going to take a one-year career break at the beginning of July 2008, as I was still being paid sick pay up until June 2008. My priorities had changed drastically and being at work was the last thing on my mind; valuable time being spent with Ruby and the family was more important.

Over the next few days, I saw a change in Ruby. I could see she was deteriorating, she was refusing to eat. I remember one day when I came to clean her mouth and could not believe what I saw. Spaghetti stored in the cheek of her mouth. How I laughed because it looked so funny but then I realised that this was from the meal she had the day before. My concern escalated. Various attempts were made to try and encourage her to eat but she was not having any of it. Despite all, we still had hope that Ruby would live and not die. No matter how bleak it looked.

Saturday 19th April 2008, I spent most of the day with Ruby but later in the evening, I went home as I needed to do a few things and I was going to church the following day. Ruby's dad stayed with her, whilst my stepdaughter and I went home. I could not settle. My mind was on Ruby the whole time. I remember phoning her dad and just checking she was fine, he said she was and encouraged me not to worry. With that, I tried my best but I could not shake off the feeling of just thinking about her. All I could do was pray and trust God that everything would be well, I would just have to hold onto God. He is not going to leave us or forsake us now. The next day, we went to church as always. I participated in worship leading, the encouraging songs kept me going. We then went to the hospital, after parking the car and just walking, I remember thinking I did not want us to be here, I just wanted us to have a normal life as a family. How much more could we take? There and then, I heard a strong clear voice, saying that we would not be here at the end of the week, we would be going home. I started to smile because I thought Ruby would be better, so we would then be able to go home. I even told my stepdaughter that we would not be here much longer.

Arriving on the ward, I could see Ruby was not too well, and noticed she did not have a feeding tube down her nose, which I had discussed with the nurse the day before and gave consent for this to be put in due to Ruby refusing to eat. I asked the nurses why it had not been done; they explained that they were not able to due to Ruby's deteriorating condition.

HOPE

By this time, I became very concerned, my motherly instinct had kicked in and I knew something was not right. I could feel it, what weren't they telling me? In the end, I just settled with Ruby. Her dad and sister left, so I was on my own, usually this did not bother me but something did not feel right. Early evening, I was lying on the bed with my gem and Ruby looked so innocent. Why did she have to go through all this pain? I could not settle at all, so I phoned my sister, Sharmaine. I was crying on the phone and shared how scared I was and she said she would come. I asked the staff member if she would be able to stay with me and they said yes, given the circumstances. When she arrived, I was so glad; I felt at ease. However, throughout the night and early hours of the next morning, I noticed Ruby's breathing becoming more labour intensive. I remember calling the nurse and explaining Ruby's symptoms, she then confirmed that her body was shutting down. Sharmaine and I looked at each other, it still did not dawn on me she was telling me my most precious JEWEL was dying. Again, I was in denial. Those next few hours seemed like eternity, I watched Ruby's every movement, kept staring at her chest to make sure it was moving up and down, so that way I knew she was still alive but you could tell it was very shallow.

Unbreak My Heart

As long as I live I will remember, Monday 21st April 2008 at approximately at 5.00 a.m., I remember screaming at the top of my lungs, when I looked across at Ruby. Alarm bells started ringing, I could not see or hear her breathing. I pressed the emergency button. Nurses and consultants came into the room and we were asked to leave. I was shaking uncontrollably, Sharmaine was trying to console me but she too was shaken and upset with what was happening, that she started vomiting. We were both in a panicked state.

It felt like eternity whilst waiting for the nurses and consultant to tell us what had happened but deep down I knew that my precious Jewel, my RUBY had transitioned. I kept thinking it was a dream. I thought that I would wake up and none of this was happening. Fifteen minutes later, they came to deliver the most devastating, heart breaking news that I would ever hear in my entire life. "Ruby has lost her fight to leukaemia and has sadly passed away." I ran to go to the Room where Ruby was, but in the middle of the corridor, I collapsed. The screams, the tears were just kept coming, they would not stop. Sharmaine too was sobbing her heart out. We both could not believe what had happened. For me, my whole world had just collapsed and gone. I did not want to live either. I wanted to die; I just wanted to be with my

HOPE

precious gem! How can life be so cruel? Where was God when I needed Him most? Why did He let this happen to us? Why my child? The why's kept on coming. At this point, my faith in God had vanished. Then suddenly, I thought of what I had heard earlier and realised it was God's voice. "You will not be in the hospital come the end of the week, you will be at home". Never did I dream that we were going home without her. I remember the staff member and my sister helping me to go into the room where Ruby lay. She was so still. I kept thinking this was a dream and it was not real but touching her and holding her still body, no sounds coming from her, I knew it was very real. The tears continued, whilst holding and rocking her, my heart felt like it was torn apart into a million pieces that couldn't be put back together again. I could barely breathe.

What am I supposed to do now? Parents don't outlive their children? Some of the nurses were crying. For them, Ruby was such a special child, I had never felt pain like this before, it was indescribable and so overwhelming. How I managed to still function is beyond me; I will never know, as I could not even call on God. I just gave up the ghost because I felt He gave up on me and left me alone to go through the most gut-wrenching situation I would ever have to face.

After a while trying to comprehend all that had happened, I knew had to make some phone calls. How do

I tell my family of this devastating news? This was one that no one would have expected. My first call was to her Dad. He could tell something was wrong, as I just kept crying; I did not want to say the words, as saying it would mean that it is true and that our precious Ruby had gone for good and I would have to accept this. I was not ready for this. Eventually, I came out with the words "Ruby has died". I could hear the echo of his voice, the cries, "no, no, no, she's not dead, she is still alive." Like me, he was in disbelief, shocked, hurting and in pain. How could this have happened? He said he would be there straightaway. My next phone calls were to my parents and siblings. They took it so hard, all were crying on the phone in disbelief and shock but encouraged me with the word of God. At that moment, to be honest, God was the last thing that I wanted to hear about but I knew they meant well. Nothing anyone said could take the pain away, as time went by, my feelings were becoming more unbearable. I did not know what to do with myself; I was going through so many emotions, guilt and regret, wondering if there was any more that we could have done? Despair and loneliness entered my mind, no one could understand what I was going through, even if they tried to, it's not the same. Feelings of extreme anger surfaced. Why did they not save her? Why did the treatment not work? Why did God let it happen to me? Why take our gem? WHY? WHY? WHY?

HOPE

Seeing Ruby just lying there, I wanted to be with her as well. I thought there was nothing to live for, if I could have taken my life there and then, I would have done anything to stop feeling the pain. Eventually, family members started to come up to the hospital and they were so torn when they saw Ruby's Dad, her sister and I; the look of disbelief on everyone's faces. The Assistant Pastor of the church came and supported and prayed for us as a family but to be honest, I felt nothing. I felt so numb, why were we praying and Ruby has gone. I felt God did not answer my prayers, so for me I wanted nothing more to do with Him, how could He allow me to be in so much pain, with my heart ripped to shreds; I was in so much internal turmoil. Ruby's dad was in a state, as for her sister, she would never hear Ruby trying to call her name or stretching her arms out for those special hugs.

Throughout the day, people kept coming and phoning, as news travelled of what had happened. I know encouragement was given to us all as a family. I had to think about the fact that Ruby was no longer in pain and she lasted longer than the Doctors had initially anticipated. She lasted just over seven weeks. Ruby definitely showed determination and fought till the end. The staff members at the hospital were so supportive and caring, letting us stay in the room until we were ready to go. I did not want to think of this. The thought of leaving our precious gem in the hospital by herself was unthinkable, even unimaginable. Who would look after her now in my absence?

After a while, I contacted my manager at work to inform her of what had happened, she too was in shock and disbelief and gave her condolences on behalf of the organisation. To be honest, all I could think about at that time, was my organisation had me in for a meeting the week before in regards to my absence. That time spent should have been quality time spent with my dying daughter and I was so angry with them for this action.

Eventually, time came when we had to pack Ruby's belongings. It was so heart-rendering, knowing that she would never use her toys again. One of her favourite toys was a stuffed green and white Giraffe, which was given to her by a couple from church. The tears flowing, blurred my vision. I thought leaving the hospital would have been a joyous day because I honestly believed that we would have left with Ruby and that she would be healed. But this was now the saddest day of my life. I was leaving the hospital feeling desperately empty, a part of me had died on that day. My heart felt so hollow inside. The tears continued flowing, seeing the faces of our families was just heart breaking, although individuals tried to console us, nothing they said could help us. I thought I would never get through this. How can we, as a family, survive this? What hope did we have? The questions kept coming but it seemed like there were no answers. Especially

HOPE

when they came to take our gem's small body to the morgue! Never did I ever think I would experience something like this or to this magnitude. We wanted our gem to wake up. This was all happening to another family, not us. It felt so surreal. Reality came when the consultant asked us to come back the following day for the death certificate. This was too much to comprehend, this journey we have never travelled. Yes, we had experienced deaths within our families, but these were adults who you expect to die. A child, this was on a totally different level, a totally new, devastating and heart-breaking experience that we were having to come to terms with. You don't expect to bury your child! Leaving the ward, I could see staff members, parents of other children, with a solemn look on their faces, some were even crying, they too realised our gem had gone, never to return!

How I managed to drive home I will never know, although other family members offered to drive, I just wanted some normality because what we experienced was not normal. Words failed us; the journey home was of silence and tears just flowing. How were we going to manage without our precious JEWEL, Ruby? All I knew was that our lives would never be the same again.

On entering our home, there was a part of us that was missing. The feeling of emptiness was so strong. I remember going inside and just falling on the floor. The tears would not stop, my heartbeat had gone. At this point, not even Ruby's dad or my stepdaughter could console me. For me, no words could take away the pain I was feeling. I just wanted my gem back! After a while, I managed to compose myself the best way I could. I tried my best to be there for Ruby's dad and her sister but this was difficult, my mind was just on Ruby. I felt guilty leaving her alone at the hospital, knowing that she was alone. I decided to go and do some shopping, in preparation for the family and friends who would visit after hearing the news. My stepdaughter came with me, she was so distressed, I tried to console and encourage her but it was hard. I knew she just could not make any sense of what had taken place. Grocery shopping is something we did on a regular basis but this time it felt abnormal. I kept thinking, 'Here we are looking normal, shopping in the store like everyone else but no one knows what we are going through'. Our hearts were so heavy.

We somehow managed to finish the shopping, return home and tidy up and cook some dinner. Everywhere we looked, there was something to remind us of Ruby: clothes, toys, her favourite foods, pictures of her and us as a family, her bathtub in our main bath. Life was unfair and so cruel. What had we done to deserve this? Where was God? In time, family and friends came around, all still in shock with what had happened, still trying to come to terms with it, all giving their condolences and encouraging us as a family to hold on to God. At one point, it just became too much, I completely broke down. I fell to the floor and sat crying and crying, the tears would not stop, my heart was in so much pain. Family and friends were holding and supporting me but all I could think of was why, God? WHY? WHY? Why did you have to take our gem, why did you not heal her?

It's only now I can answer these questions and say that God gives and takes life away, no matter the age, gender, colour, religion, no one is exempt. It's a journey that we all have to travel someday, and some will go before others. Through the evening, more and more family and friends visited and it was nice to have such support. Eventually, we had a time of prayer, although I knew we needed it as a family, to be honest, I could not feel anything, prayer was the last thing on my mind but we were grateful for the support from all. After everyone had left, it was us by ourselves. I remember laying on the bed with my stepdaughter and she was crying; she shared with me that everyone she had ever loved had died. She and her dad had gone through loss of loved ones over the years, her grandparents, uncles but nothing had compared to this loss of her special sister, Ruby. All I could do was reassure her the best way I knew how.

Eventually we all went to bed but I could not sleep, I tossed and turned, over and over my mind was on Ruby, flashbacks of her passing in my arms, kept coming to me. I could not wait for the next morning to come, as I knew we would be busy. The next day arrived, I was hoping that this would be a dream but seeing Ruby's cot empty, I knew it was real. We had arranged to return to the hospital to collect the death certificate and go and visit our gem in the chapel of rest. We were not looking forward to this but knew it had to be done. Arriving to collect the death certificate was just so surreal. How can we be collecting a death certificate for a seventeen-month-old child, when it wasn't long ago we were registering her birth? It was too difficult to comprehend! We then went to the chapel of rest, our gem was already prepared for viewing. I was so scared, thinking what she would look like? Her body was cold, however she looked like she was a sleeping beauty. I wanted to take her home but knew this would never happen. As the tears flowed, we managed to say our goodbyes. Ruby's dad then left to go and register her death, I said I did not wish to go with him, it would be too difficult. My stepdaughter and I returned home. We just sat and reflected what we had just gone through. Another new heart-wrenching experience for us, which I would not wish on anyone. We both felt guilty that we had to leave our gem at the hospital but what could we do? Family and friends continued to visit; at times I just went upstairs to my bedroom, as I just wanted to be myself, which is understandable. No words would bring her back to me.

No Parent Should Have to Bury Their Child

My life was a big, hazy blur however, I remember this day clearly; Wednesday 23rd April 2008, we went to a few funeral directors to look at planning our gem's funeral! How do you choose a casket for your child? The staff members at the co-op funeral directors were friendly, sensitive, sympathetic and helpful. Obviously, they were trained to deal with this but we were not prepared. Talking about hearses, cars for the family, wreaths, flowers, horse and carriage, choice of cemetery, time of service, felt like the staff members were speaking another language to me. I just wanted to go home, because this was becoming more and more of a reality, every day I lived. I felt like I was in denial and kept thinking I would wake up and it would have been a dream. The tears flowed for us, it was so distressing. Thankfully my dad and my brother in-law, Rob, were with Ruby's Dad and I, so they helped us to make some choices regarding our gem's celebration of life service. I can never thank them enough.

We confirmed with our Pastor, who was also Ruby's God father, that the service will be held on Thursday 1st May 2008 at our local church. I thought, 'This is just over a week away. I do not think I can do this, I can't bury my child.' Before leaving, the funeral parlour confirmed they

HOPE

would go to the hospital the following day, to collect our gem's body.

I was so glad, as I thought she would be nearer to us for visiting but even so this was not what I wanted. We would have given anything to have our precious jewel back with us. Over the next few days, we had more and more family and friends visiting, mainly bringing food that they had prepared, which we were so grateful for, as we did not have the strength to cook every day. There were phone calls from others, particularly those who were overseas. Often there were times when I did not want to speak to anyone at all, so I stayed in my bedroom, just reflecting on what had happened and what we were going through as a family. This whole situation was so unfair. It just did not seem right. Also, over the next few days, we spent time arranging the funeral programme. Who would give tributes, songs, a dance to be done to our gem's favourite song: HOSANNA, by Kirk Franklin. We all thought this would have to be done by her cousin, Dom. We all agreed that we would ask people to wear the colours pink and white. We really did want this to be a celebration of Ruby's life. I then thought about what clothes would I bury my gem in?

My stepdaughter and I went into town one day to TK Maxx and we saw a beautiful pink dress; I remember when I got to the till, the cashier who served me commented on how beautiful the dress was and asked who was it for? I responded my daughter, she then asked, "is it for a party?" At that point I became so overwhelmed, I did not know what to say. I did not respond. I could not. It dawned on me, to others we may just look like a normal mother and child shopping but no one had a clue that our hearts were eternally broken.

Upon returning home, I informed Ruby's dad of what we had experienced and he tried to encourage us. Over the next few days, Ruby's dad and step-sister went to the chapel of rest to see our precious jewel! I could not attend. I did not want to. I did not want to be reminded of what I was going through. It was coming up to the weekend and I just wanted to block it all out. I had made up in my mind that I was not going to church that Sunday. However, on the morning, Ruby's dad encouraged us all to go as a family, as he said we needed the strength of our church family. I was reluctant at first but eventually decided to go. Although my body was present during the service, my mind was elsewhere. I kept thinking in a few days, I would be burying my gem and her celebration of life service would be held at our local church. All prayers and encouragement were given to us; we were able to inform all of the impending service and that we would like all attending to wear the colours, pink and white. As much as I was glad to be in church because it was a different environment, I just wanted to go home.

The next few days were difficult, putting the final touches to the programme, contacting individuals who would be involved on the day, also writing our gem's eulogy. This was extremely difficult but as a family, we did it together and put our own personal thoughts to it. Wow. It should be the child writing their parents' eulogy and not the other way around. As time drew nearer to our gem's celebration of life service, I was becoming more and more anxious. Family members were worried about me, even I was worried about myself. I was not sleeping; I had very little sleep in the last week and half. I had to go to the doctor and get some sedatives. It was not what I wanted but right now there was no choice, I needed to try and sleep, to avoid collapsing from exhaustion.

The day before our dear gem's celebration of life service, I went to have my hair done by my regular hairdresser, whilst Ruby's dad and her sister went to the chapel of rest to dress Ruby in the clothes I had prepared. There was no way that I could have done this. The final ending drew nearer and I was still in denial that she was just asleep and would soon wake up and she would be at home again. I wanted that so badly. Whilst at the hairdresser, I remember being so quiet. I did not say much. My mind was thinking about what would be taking place the following day. How in God's name was I and the rest of the family going to get through the day? I remember my hairdresser asking me what was the occasion for me having my hair done. When I told her of

Ruby's passing and her celebration of life service was the next day, I could see her eyes welling up. All she could do was give her condolences because no amount of words could change the level of pain that I was experiencing. On returning home, I remembered that the funeral directors would be bringing our dear Ruby's body home later that day, as we had decided to have her body overnight at our home to say one final goodbye. To be honest, I was so reluctant to do this but Ruby's dad had requested for this to be done as part of his culture; in fact, I remember we had argued about this. It was only after the celebration of life service, that I realised that it was the right thing to do, as this prepared me and the family for the next day, in giving us strength to cope and just being able to spend our final hours with our precious gem.

I remember when the funeral directors arrived with the tiny casket, I just broke down immediately. I felt so weak in the knees. My baby, my poor baby. Some of the neighbours were looking in disbelief, as she arrived. It was such a devastating and painful experience. 'Will we ever get through this?', I wondered? The funeral directors put the casket in the living room, it was left open; how she looked so beautiful, like a little angel. We knew family and friends would be visiting later to pay their final respects and to give encouragement to us, as a family. For me, I still found it difficult to have her body in the house, so I spent most of the time upstairs in my bedroom. There were times when I did view my gem's body. I touched and kissed her on a few occasions. The morning of her celebration of life service came. It dawned on me that we were going to bury our precious jewel! This would be our final farewell, we would never have the opportunity to see her again in this lifetime. I cried buckets of tears that day.

My heart was crumbling into a million pieces. How was I going to get through this day? We all managed to get ready, I don't think there was a dry eye in the house. How this was so traumatic, the pain was excruciating. I did not want to bury my child. No parent should have to do this, I had no choice in the matter, I just had to put one foot in front of the other.

The funeral directors had arrived. I stood still, because seeing the white horses and carriage, and the funeral cars, suddenly made everything so final. I felt such an agonizing pain in my chest. After the funeral directors placed Ruby's casket in the carriage, and all family members got into the funeral cars, the journey that none of us wanted had started. It felt like a lifetime. I could see bystanders looking on. Their facial expressions said what we were all feeling inside. It was too painful, heart-rending and felt so unfair, that my daughter had died. The tears poured like a river. I was in disbelief. My family tried to console me but no amount of words could help, no one was feeling the pain I felt. As a mother, to bring a child into the world and then to bury the same child, was too unimaginable. On arrival at our church, I told myself this was a bad dream and surely, I would wake up soon, reality cannot be avoided. My legs almost gave way as I watched the undertakers remove our precious gem's casket from the carriage. After composing ourselves, the best we could, with the undertaker walking ahead with the small white casket, Ruby's dad, her sister and I followed hand in hand, then we were followed by the rest of family and friends. We walked into our local Church. About five years ago, we got married at the church, but now we were here for our gem, Ruby's celebration of life service. Why was life so cruel?

Walking in and seeing all the solemn faces was just too much for me. Yes, we were there to celebrate the short life of a unique, beautiful child! Sadness lingered in the walls of the church. No one could take away that excruciating pain that we were feeling as a family. I wanted the service to stop but I knew that could not happen. Throughout the service, I kept my eyes fixed on Ruby's minute casket. I wished that she would have woken up. I would have done anything to see that happen or trade places. I wished with all my heart but God had the final say and wanted her home more. Even though at the time, I did not agree with her premature death. I was very angry, enraged in fact. Why take my young baby? So many people came to pay their respects, even many of the staff members from the hospital. The church was full to the brim. I said a silent prayer, "God, please just get me through today." Ruby's godfather was the officiating minister for the service. He had done many funerals but I knew this one was hard because of the personal connection.

As the service carried on, there were so many tributes and songs in memory of our gorgeous Ruby. All were so lovely and I knew some found it difficult, just as we did as a family. My favourites were a dance by my niece, Dominique, to the song, 'Hosanna' by Kirk Franklin, Ruby's favourite song. Ruby danced to this each morning, clapping her hands and smiling. Another favourite was a tribute by my sisters, Zena, Carol and Sharmaine. The songs they sang were so fitting, 'Weeping may endure for a night, but joy comes in the morning'; 'I just can't give up now, I've come too far from where I've started from, nobody told me that road would be easy, I don't believe He's brought me this far to leave me.' Although the words of these songs were so comforting, my heart remained broken.

In a few moments, we will be laying our precious babygirl to rest. How were we going to cope afterwards? It was going to be so hard. Ruby's dad read the eulogy. That felt so unreal, I don't how he managed to do this. I remember standing with him for support; it was an emotional time, something that will remain with us forever. Towards the end of the service, we had Ruby's tiny casket opened for all to view. How she looked immaculate, just like an angel. She looked like she was sleeping. As individuals were paying their last respects and whilst passing us, as the immediate family, they gave their condolences. Although I was grateful for their words of encouragement, my mind was elsewhere. I kept my eyes fixed on the tiny white casket, knowing that it would soon be closed forever. I would never in this life see my baby again. Only in heaven! Our final moments with our beloved daughter were now coming to an end. I could not believe this was happening, I remember we had placed some special mementos in her casket. A family picture, a small stuffed toy and a bible. We said our goodbyes one last time to our Ruby. I kissed her gently. Saying the final goodbye was so difficult. How the tears flowed. This was the final journey to the cemetery. I knew that we would be returning home without her.

As we arrived, watching her dad carry her tiny casket to the grave was heart-rending. My body felt like it was going to explode. I cried and I cried. My mum and stepdaughter walked with me. I felt like I was going to collapse. The tears never stopped, they always cry on the inside of me. I can't do this. How can I watch them bury my whole world? All my hope had gone. My world shattered, like glass hitting the ground. My heart wounded and battered. How would I put the pieces back together again? Would I ever smile again? No. How could I? As the undertakers lowered the tiny casket into the

HOPE

grave, I wanted to go into the grave and take it back out. I put a single pink rose in the grave. Family members and friends began to mould up the grave. Various songs were sung, some in Lingala, which was Ruby's dad's language. This was definitely a celebration of Ruby's precious life.

After finally putting all the flowers on the grave, there were so many, final prayers were said. It was the most horrific day that I would experience in my life and this part was now over. I stood by the grave for what seemed like forever, I did not want to leave my angel by herself. But deep down, I knew she was safe in the arms of Jesus. This was the hardest thing that I had ever done or experienced. Everyone continued to comment on how beautiful the service was. For one of my cousins, he said this was the best celebration of life service that he had ever been to. As much as it was a beautiful celebration of such a unique life, to me it was every parent's worst nightmare, to bury your child. Will I survive? Will we survive? How can there be any hope from this?

The day followed with refreshments at the Emerald Club. Ruby's dad and I were commended as a couple, for the strength we had shown throughout the day. I did not feel strong but I knew that I had not broken down as much as I thought I would have. There were times when I could not help but shed tears. I remember going to use the facilities at the Emerald and I found myself just crying and looking at a picture of my gem, which was given to me earlier in the day, by a close friend. Why did you have to go? My sister, Zena, saw me and she just hugged me. Thank you Sis. I really did not know what I was going to do after all this. As much as this day was real, I did not want it to be. Later on in the evening, after most people had gone and we had collected all the sympathy cards, we returned home. The house felt so desolate and cold, without Ruby's warm smile. It was evident someone was missing. I went straight upstairs and sat on the bed and made up for the tears that I had not cried before.

It had to come out. I felt so alone. Yes, there was family around me but they could not take away the pain inside; my smile had left me. As long as I live, I would never want to bury another child. This experience was just too much to bear and handle. Returning home without Ruby, felt like life had ended. Things could never be the same. That evening, we discussed about going away for a few days, as a family. I knew we needed a change of scenery, which would do us all good.

As night came, I could not sleep; in fact, I did not want to sleep because I felt that if I did go to sleep it would have to be forever, as I did not want to wake up. All I wanted was to be with my beautiful baby girl. I just laid there, reflecting on the whole day and the last few weeks. Thinking of life without my precious gem was unbearable. How do parents come back from this? How would we as a family, come back from this? The next day came, we decided as a family that we wanted to go and visit Ruby's grave. It was an attempt to come to terms with what had happened. I remember when we arrived, I just wanted to dig the grave up.

There were so many flowers over the grave. I knew that we were still in disbelief that we had gone through this. We had our own little private service, singing choruses and praying and declaring our love and how much we miss our Ruby. I spent the rest of the day booking Ruby's dad, her sister and I, a trip to Brighton for a few days. We were looking forward to this. Whilst packing, it dawned on me that there was someone missing and we could not change it. We would just have to try to cope and adjust our lives. There was such an empty void that needed filling; this was so upsetting and saddening but what could we do about it?

I contacted family members to inform them that we would be away for a few days. They were glad for us. I got up quite early, as we were travelling by coach. The journey down to Brighton was fine; we did not do much talking as a family. I personally think we were just trying to cope individually, the best way we could. We all thought of the same thing, our precious gem, Ruby is missing and she should have been with us. Even then, I still felt this feeling of isolation, I just felt that no one could understand how I was truly feeling, as a mother.

HOPE

On arrival, it was nice to be in different scenery to take our minds off the last few days, weeks and months. However, it was impossible to relax, as Ruby was thought of every minute. She was always in my thoughts. After unpacking, we decided to go out for a meal; to others, we looked like a normal family but they could not be further from the truth. How could we be normal? We had just buried our angel. We tried our best to try to enjoy our time away but I did not at all. I wanted my baby back.

Her dad had a lot of things bottled up and even trying to talk about what we had gone through was hard. They say experiences that we go through as a family either break us or make us stronger. I knew this was going to break us. Although it was nice to be by the seaside, there were times I went for a walk down by the pier, in solitude. For the rest of the time and for the sake of my stepdaughter, I tried to participate as much as I could. For me nothing would ever be the same again. Eventually, we returned home. Again, that empty void followed us there, also.

New Normal

Eventually Ruby's dad returned to work. I still had not returned; I did not think I could cope with work at this point. My stepdaughter had returned to school. I could see the emptiness in her eyes, I knew she missed her sister so much. We all just wanted Rubees back. I tried my best to be the mother that she needed at that time but this was a lot, as I was in mourning and going through the grieving process. I felt I needed someone to be totally there for me but I did not feel that I could turn to anyone, not even Ruby's dad. We began drifting apart, I supposed her death was the tip of the iceberg and I could feel that. I had so many emotions. I knew I needed to get professional support.

Ruby's godfather advised that, as a family, we have bereavement counselling. At first I was reluctant, people's perception of counselling is that you are crazy. In the end, I knew that it was needed. Several counsellors in our church organisation were recommended but I did not want that, as I explained that I needed to be myself and did not think I could do that with someone I knew. So, I decided to go through my doctor. Now I know that was the best decision I had made. Ruby's dad decided that he did not want counselling. I know this was part of being a man and his culture. Ruby's sister decided she wanted to have counselling. I contacted my doctor and I was seen by a nurse, who obviously felt my heartache and after going through a number of questions, gave me contact details for a few bereavement counselling services. I decided to wait a few days before making any contact. The day arrived, firstly, I contacted one service by phone but I did not feel anything, so I contacted another organisation by phone and immediately I connected with the person taking the call, they were so friendly and gave me reassurance. Most of all, they supported families who had lost a child. I knew immediately this was the one.

The first session was set up for myself and stepdaughter for the following week and I was so glad, as I believed we were going to receive the support we needed in helping us to understand our emotions and help us to cope with the devastation that we were experiencing in our lives. I did some research online, about the organisation and this confirmed my choice. The day arrived that we were due to attend and on entering and going to reception, again that friendly manner and homeliness greeted us. We were asked to sit in the waiting area and complete a registration form, giving brief details of our bereavement.

I sat and observed individuals in the room, some with solemn and sad facial expressions. Well, as I thought about the reason why we were there, surely it was not a happy one. I did not know what to expect from the session, as I never had counselling before. This was a whole new experience for us both. After a short wait, my stepdaughter and I were called by a female counsellor. We were guided to a small room on the next floor. On entering, it felt so calm and relaxing. The counsellor introduced herself and asked us to do the same; she explained about the services on offer by the organisation and I felt so over whelmed but I knew deep down we both needed this. She explained that the sessions would be weekly and after this initial session, my stepdaughter and I would be seen separately. We were both in agreement, although we were both grieving, we were coping with it differently, so I believed this would help us immensely to try and cope the best way we could.

The counsellor asked me to give brief details of our grief! Where do I start from was my initial thought, how do you explain something so raw and devastating? This was going to be hard, I looked at my stepdaughter. As the tears began to stream down my face, I explained the loss of our beautiful gem and how it was so heart-breaking. When my Ruby's sister expressed some of her feelings: scared, alone, confused, why did this happen?, it was so saddening as I could feel that she too was hurting and struggling, trying to come to terms with the loss of her sibling. Of course, this would be difficult for any fifteen-year-old to deal with. As we came to end of the session, I felt it was just good to be able to express myself and just be me without judgement. I did not have to put on a front. I was able to grieve freely, with no expectations. I asked my stepdaughter how she felt about the session, she said it was useful and that she wanted to continue with the sessions on a one-to-one basis. Deep down, I knew we needed this. It was going to be a long process, but with God, I knew He would see me through.

Each and every day was a time of reflection. I thought about the preceding year and what had actually taken place and at times, it was too much to comprehend. There were days when I wished that it was all a very bad dream and everything was fine but the reality was that we were going through such a difficult time as a family, things would never be the same. To me, the anchor of our family had gone, her short life had so much impact on others and she was no longer around. Life was so unfair. Having that short motherhood experience of my own biological child, was just devastating, the pain that it left was indescribable. Even to this very day, at times I still question it but I have learned to accept that it is the will of God and I may never really understand why.

Although my stepdaughter and I continued with counselling sessions, Ruby's dad did not wish to attend, even though I could see he was struggling with his emotions and believed that the counselling would have really helped him. I accepted that everyone grieves differently and had to respect that. During my sessions, I started to feel more and more comfortable with my counsellor. Each time, it became easier to say exactly how I was feeling, which I felt helped, as it made me understand myself in regards to my emotions and the grieving process. After about the fifth session, I remember my counsellor saying to me, that she is picking up that I keep saying that no one understands how I am feeling. I informed her that is how I felt, that no one could understand, I lost my beautiful baby. Not my family or friends could understand, as much as they tried to, for me they could not, I did not want them to understand either, as I would not wish that excruciating pain on anyone.

I did not want others to feel what I was feeling. My counsellor said she wanted to share her own personal experience with me and she was waiting for the right time and felt this was it. At this point, I was curious in what she would be sharing with me. I was left with a puzzled look on my face, as she could identify 100% with what I'd been going through. I remember just looking in a state of shock and then the tears started to flow from my eyes; I began to thank God, I thought she definitely knew what I was going through. God is so awesome, He saw my need and sent me to the right counsellor. Oh, how I gave my condolences.

She further explained that her loss was one of the main reasons she came into this work because at the time of her loss, counselling service was not available and it was her faith in God that had kept her and she wanted to give back to others. Not only did God choose a counsellor who had gone through the same experience but also one who was a Christian. What an amazing God we serve. I could see the benefits of the sessions for both my stepdaughter and I, as we slowly began to cope, taking each day and each moment at a time. We continued with life, trying to do normal things but at the back and the forefront of my mind and deep in my heart, Ruby was thought of always and how her presence was missed so much.

Eventually in July 2008, I returned to work, on reduced hours and days for the first eight weeks. Even though I did not really want to go back to work, I knew I needed to get back into routine and to keep my mind occupied. The first day on the 9th, I was so emotional. It dawned on me that it was a year since Ruby was first diagnosed with leukaemia. The tears flowed whilst I was at my desk; I remember my colleague consoling me and asking me if I wanted to go home but I decided to stay, as hard as it was. The date flooded my mind with memories of that awful day but with God I knew that He would continue to see me through difficult days like this, as He has done. My workplace was supportive; they knew I was still going through a difficult time. Slowly, I began to settle into a routine of going to work, being a stepmother, a wife, being with family and friends. Between you and me, it was all too much to deal with.

I just could not shake off the feeling. No one understands. Yes, my counselling sessions helped but outside of those, it was difficult. I felt that people expected me to be the same person that I was before Ruby passed. As for me that was not the case, I would never be the same person, as long as I lived. How could I be, after the experience I had gone through? I know individual lives had to go on but mine was a different life. Even family events were not the same, as there was one precious little person missing and even today, that still remains the same for me. Sometimes, the expectation to be at certain events was too much, such as birthdays, anniversaries, funerals etc. Initially, I could not cope. I remember during one of my counselling sessions, mentioning this to my counsellor. Her advice was; don't put yourself in a position that you don't wish to be in because after the event, when you return home, no one sees your heartache or pain and you have to deal with this. I really reflected on what she said and to this day, I follow that advice given.

As time went by, the family unit became more distant, relationships became strained, in particular with Ruby's dad. Communication between us had gradually broken down, as much as I tried as a wife to improve our relationship, it was too much, with underlying issues, we eventually split up. How I was so devastated. Losing my child and not long after, my marriage. How was I ever going to cope? Only with God! I felt so broken, where do I go now?

HOPE

I know now, that it has been God's strength that has kept me so far. Again, I just felt like totally giving up. My stepdaughter decided she wanted to stay with me. At first, I did not have a problem, because I knew she needed stability, love and reassurance that she was not on her own. She was a teenager who was going through an extremely difficult time, so I felt I needed to be there for her. Although I wanted and needed someone to be there for me too but I knew I had to put my own feelings aside and concentrated on those that needed me the most. It was not easy, things were fine at first but after about six months, things began to change. The relationship between us broke down and she went to stay with her dad. My initial reaction was shock and devastation. A whole family broken within a year. I just could not comprehend what had happened.

Even questioning God. How can this be the will for my life? Losing my family? As much as I tried to put on a front, I did not want to live, what was the point? I just could not see a reason to live at this point, I just felt I was in complete darkness. The person I most missed, was my delightful Ruby. I felt my heart was just crumbling to pieces, and no one, no matter how hard they tried, could put the pieces back together again. Too many losses in a short space of time, my mind was all over the place again.

Dealing with particular events, for example, Christmas without Ruby, was practically unbearable. Seeing my siblings with their children, as they opened up their presents, was too much. I remember one time just going into the kitchen and I just cried and cried, the tears were unstoppable. I wanted Ruby to be there also, so I could watch her opening presents too but I would never see this again. Heartbreak was an understatement. No words could sufficiently describe the pain I felt. My family tried to console me but no matter what they did, the feeling remained. I felt at an all-time low, despite continuing with counselling sessions. I was still taking antidepressants and sleeping tablets.

To me, life looked so bleak. What was the point of carrying on? I remember one day being at home, the tears falling down my face; I could not take it anymore. I surely did not want to live. I entertained thoughts of, 'Why don't you end your life?' Well, why not? There was no reason in living. Yes, I had my parents and siblings but I wanted my little girl back and with everything else that had gone on, it felt like the only option was to end it all. How could I carry on? I remember one evening, I sat in the living room and began texting my family goodbye messages. I then took around ten paracetamol tablets. My life was over. Knowing now the word of God says, 'I shall not die, but live and declare the works of the Lord' Amen! Apart from having a really bad headache, I was physically fine. My family learnt what I had tried to do and were shocked but gave me that extra support that I needed. A big thank you all to them all for keeping me here.

I decided to go away. In May 2009, I went to Nevis for two weeks and spent time again with my uncle and auntie. I needed that secluded time away from everything and was grateful for this. On my return, I decided to take time out, I had some time on sick leave from my work and time away from church. I remember my parents thinking I had given up on God. To some degree they were right, I just could not understand why I had gone through so much. I just wanted to be by myself. My immediate family, I communicated with but anyone else I did not want to know. I received so many text and email messages checking how I was doing but I did not respond. I just wanted some 'me' time and God time. And I did in isolating myself, time of reflection, just thinking and asking God, how could I make it through this? I did not know what was going to happen and what the outcome would be regarding my life but deep down, I knew I had to try to hold on. Over time, I began to slowly feel better within myself and eventually I was able to re-develop my relationship with God. I returned to work and to church. I knew God would equip me to cope each and every day and I was getting to know God on a different level. It's so easy to praise God when everything is going well but to do that in the toughest of circumstances of one's life, is the real challenge for anyone. We have to learn and demonstrate that in every situation, we should

HOPE

give thanks to God. At times, we forget what God is able to do for us but in everything, we should give Him thanks and the praise because that's what He deserves.

Hope, Glory and God

As time went by, I gradually realised I was getting to a better place, emotionally and spiritually. This gave me reassurance and hope, feeling that eventually I was going to be alright. Yes, it is a long process and I still have a way to go, 'All things are possible in God' for example, it was possible to smile and laugh again, guilt-free. Despite going through a blizzard of non-existence, there was a glimmer of hope in God and that He had not forgotten me. I could see the light seeping through the dark clouds, which I did not think I would ever see, after such a shattering loss. I could hear the birds tweet again. Yes, my faith at times was like a mustard seed and has been tested to the max but I was determined to hold onto God, no matter what. I related heavily to a beautiful song Kurt Carr's, "I Almost Let Go".

Verse 1

I almost let go

I felt like I couldn't take life anymore

My problems had me bound

Depression weighed me down

But God held me close

So, I wouldn't let go

HOPE

God's mercy Kept me

So, I wouldn't let go

I almost gave up

I was right on the edge of a breakthrough

But couldn't see it

The devil really had me

But Jesus came and grabbed me

And He held me close,

So, I wouldn't let go.

God's mercy kept me,

So, I wouldn't let go

Kurt Carr – All music

To be honest, sometimes I felt like giving up and taking the easy way out, by ending my life. For me, my life would never be the same again but I realise that would have been selfish of me. That feeling of emptiness and loneliness enveloped me on a daily basis, which was a painful thing to deal with. God helped me to cope. God showed that during this awful time, He had never left me, He was by my side the whole time, even when I could not see or feel it, He was always there.

HOPE

Isaiah 41:10 confirms this. 'Fear not for I am with you; Be not dismayed, for I am your God. I will strengthen you, Yes, I will help you, I will uphold you with my righteous hand.' God is so true to His words. He has upheld me. Thank you, God, so much. I could have gone under but here I am still standing, in spite of the pain, the storm and the rain, I stand in His strength alone.

God wants us to believe and trust in Him. He knows what He is doing, even if you cannot make sense of things that may have happened or are taking place now, He is the all-powerful God. Even when I could not understand the loss of my one and only child, I accept that God gives and He takes away life. He did not say how long each of us would live, some will have a short life and others longer and that's the way it is. My precious Ruby had a short life but she was blessed to make such an impact on myself and others in that short time and for that, I will be eternally grateful. She will never be forgotten; her memory and legacy will live on. There are times I still question WHY? That is the human side, nevertheless I understand that she is no longer suffering in that terrible pain, she is in a better place - in the arms of GOD!

Sometime after Ruby had passed, I began to look at how I could get back into the church activity, for example, going to church on a regular basis, as I had stopped going; so for me it was about taking one day at a time. It was through God's strength, He allowed me to do this and first it was not easy, as time went by it became easier. I felt that I had a purpose, despite the earth-shattering experience God had a plan, I believed that God was going to allow me to use this experience to help others. True to His word, He did. I remember being appointed as youth and cell group leader, I thought, 'God you're funny!'. I wondered, how could I do this? I am not at that place to be able to give of myself. God had a different plan. There were also times I was able to share my testimony.

On one occasion, I remember being asked to speak; the Theme at the time was 'Praising God through difficult times.' At first, I thought not to do it but then thinking to myself, if anyone can do this, I can. I had no choice, I could not keep this to myself, I had to let others know that in spite of tragic situations, there was Hope. Recognising I had and still experienced tribulations but was able to praise God in harrowing circumstances. I remember that Sunday when I shared about the last few months and how hard it had been and even saying that, although I had been a Christian at that time for twenty years or so, I thought I knew God. However, it had been in the months whilst being in hospital, when Ruby received her treatment and then her passing, that I really got to know God and my relationship with Him had deepened. Feedback from others was that I encouraged them to keep holding on to God, no matter what. It was after sharing my testimony in church, that I realised this is where I need to be and God would be opening up opportunities for me to inspire others and in all of this, His name would be glorified.

Despite what you may go through in life, for example loss of loved ones, family and friends who forget about you, loss of your marriage, home, job, also financial difficulties, or diagnosed with a terminal illness, you cannot give up! You must not give up! God is with you always! He is the only person that can take you through any situation. God brought me out from the darkest place I have ever been, all I could do was depend on Him, cry out to Him. I did not think that I would have been alive today but if He can do that for me, He is able to do it for you too.

We must realise that our tests are a testimony for others, amen. I will always share my experience, strength and hope. It is so important to do so; you will never know whose life you will touch.

Another opportunity to share my experience came in 2011; I had enrolled on a counselling course, as I thought in time, I would like to become a professional counsellor. One of our assignments was to write about why we decided to undertake the course. We had a few weeks to prepare, which we then would share with the rest of the group. I based my reasons on the passing of my gem, Ruby, I remember writing it with tears in my eyes, as memories surfaced. On that day, I was feeling very nervous but God was with me. There were four us who were allocated time to share, two of the group members went before me and there was opportunity given for questions and answers after they had finished. Then my turn came and as I started to read, I could sense the room was so quiet, you could hear a pin drop. By the time I had finished reading, literally the whole group and the male tutor was in tears and even I was emotional.

No one had any questions as they felt it said what it needed to say. After class had finished, the tutor commended me for sharing and how it was so touching. For me, that was the highlight of the course. I was proud of what I had achieved, even weeks later, other students shared with me that my story was just so touching; they shared my pain and empathy and said the courage I showed was unbelievable. If they had gone through that experience, they would not have been able to let others hear what they had gone through. You will never know what you are capable of, until life slaps you in the face.

There have been times where I have shared my experience at women's conferences, in my workplace, with family and friends, sharing my inner heart-felt thoughts. I have also responded to an article of a problem page in a daily newspaper, where a mother had written she was on the verge of suicide, after the loss of her child. The editor responded back and thanked me for sharing my experience.

HOPE

We don't know whose lives we will touch with our life experiences but we must know that what we go through, is not in vain but for a purpose. Situations may be unmanageable and sorrowful at times and yes, we do not like what we may have gone through or are still going through. All we can do is allow God to carry us through, we can show others there is always HOPE!

My darling Ruby continues to be my strength and inspiration to keep me going in spirit, to fight, no matter what and to never, ever give up. Don't get me wrong, I still have difficult moments, especially on days like Mother's Day, seeing other children appreciating their mothers. Knowing that if Ruby was with us, she would be doing the same, has meant that every Mother's Day since her passing, I go through an emotional rollercoaster. Just seeing my nieces and nephews growing up, I love them all dearly, however for me, I always think there is one person missing. My gem! Other events remain difficult at times, attending children's parties, seeing other children perform in my local church, attending funerals, especially of a child or young person, it can be difficult. However, God has taught me that in every situation, He helps you to cope, there is a way through, and He will not leave you on your own to deal with it, as long as you believe and trust in Him. He has your back, He gives you the tools and equipment to cope with every situation; yes life can be tough but God is faithful till the end. Be hopeful in all you do. They say

HOPE

time is a great healer, through this life-changing experience, I can say that it does get easier as time goes by. Grief is a process that if we live long enough, we all will experience. I want you to know that it does become less distressing, know that you are not on your own, God almighty is covering you at all times and comforting you, be reassured of this. Also know that our situations are not for a lifetime, they are for a SEASON!

Scriptures and Prayers of Encouragement

The following scriptures and prayers are to help you in your time of need. It may not be that you are facing this type of situation, however you could be entering a dark valley in your life. Use it to help uplift you spirit and know that Jesus is the King of Kings and the Lord of Lords.

"It is the Lord who goes before you. He will be with you; He will not leave you or forsake you. Do not fear or be dismayed".

Deuteronomy 31:8

"Even though I walk through the valley of shadow of death, I will fear no evil, for you are with me; your rod and staff they comfort me."

Psalm 23:4

"I can do all things through Christ who strengthens me." Hebrews 6:19: *"HOPE anchors the soul."*

Philippians 4:13

John 14:27 (NKJV): *"Peace I leave with you, my peace I give to you; not as the world gives do I give to you. Let not your heart be troubled, neither let it be afraid."*

Matthew 5:4 (NKJV): Blessed are those who mourn, for they shall be comforted.

Jeremiah 29:11 (NKJV): *For I know the thought I think toward you, says the Lord, thoughts of peace and not of evil, to give you a future and a hope.*

Isaiah 43:2 (NKJV): *When you pass through the waters, I will be with you; And through the rivers, they shall not overflow you. When you walk through the fire, you shall not be burned, Nor shall the flame scorch you.*

Revelation 21:4 (NKJV): *"And God will wipe away every tear from their eyes; there shall be no more death, no more sorrow, nor more crying. There shall be no more pain, for the former things have passed away.*

Prayer 1

Lord here I am, right now I don't know what to say, my whole world has gone, I need your help and strength right now, please help me God!

Amen!

Prayer 2

Dear Lord it's me! I feel so broken and in despair right now. How can I get through the night? My life will never be the same again.

HOPE

My beautiful Angel has gone, reveal to me, through words, thoughts and deeds the reason why they left.

I really can't make sense of what has happened, comfort me oh Lord. Help me!

The loss of any child is heart breaking, Lord what am I going to do? I just feel like giving up, I need your guidance to help me cope.

I know you won't give me more than I can bear, but right now it seems so unbearable. I am not sure of what to do now

But help me to take one moment at a time and to pray and meditate day and night on your word.

Your word says in **Psalm 23:1 The Lord is my shepherd I shall not want.**

Help me to know that your grace is sufficient and that you will never leave me.

Amen!

Prayer 3

Lord, as I come to you now, I am so lost for words, my tears, only you understand and my pain, only you can heal.

I don't know what to do, I feel so isolated in a crowded room, only you understand what I am going through?

HOPE

Help me God and show me how can I get through this? It is so hard. I know I must bow my bended knees before thee and take it one day at time, the pain will get easier, and I know Lord you will be with me every step of the way.

You are my light, you are my love, you are my strength, you teach me that there is enough HOPE to heal the word!

Let me be your humble servant all the days of my life and share with the world the message that you are King of Kings, Lord of Lords, there is no one greater.

Amen!

Ten Favourite Songs

1. I almost let go – Kirk Carr
2. My life is in your hands – Kirk Franklin
3. Hosanna – Kirk Franklin (Ruby's Favourite Song)
4. Never would have made it without you – Marvin Sapp
5. You are my strength – Hillsong
6. You made a way – Travis Greene
7. Still – Hillsong
8. Jesus keep me near the cross – Bishop Carlton Pearson
9. Jesus loves me – Whitney Houston
10. Because He lives, I can face tomorrow – Benita Jones

Epilogue

We may not know what the future holds, despite our brokenness, disappointments, joys and fears but we know who holds our future. Never give up on God, because He does not give up on us. He is our 'HOPE' in all things; remember things that happen in life are inevitable.

Psalm 30:5 "Weeping may endure for a night, but joy comes in the morning."

I am grateful to God that I did not give up during those heart-breaking times because I would not have the privilege of being able to write this book to help others. Yes, life is tough sometimes and it can be so unfair; holding on is hard, it can be impossible but know that God is faithful till the end, no matter how hopeless life gets. He will fight for us always. You can count on Him to walk beside you because He loves you. God will never allow us to suffer beyond our own capabilities. There is nothing on this earth more certain than 'HOPE' in God. He is our anchor for the present and the future. Can God trust you to hold on? All we have to do is take a leap of faith and 'HOPE' in God for the things we cannot see.

'I praise You and worship You, Lord. I love You and recognise that all I have is from You. Everything I have is

Yours, and I surrender it all to You for Your glory. Therefore, whatever I have lost, I release into Your hands. I praise You and thank You that this is the day that You have made, so I will rejoice and be glad in it. Thank You for Your grace and mercy.   Thank You loving me the way You do. Thank You for bringing good out of my situation. No matter what has happened or will happen in my life, as long as I am alive, I will sing, eternally sing Your praises.'

The following scriptures are to sustain you and keep you going through the storms of life.

Psalm 146 v 1-2.

This book is a reminder for all that even in your darkest hour, or your most heart-breaking moment, there is HOPE in GOD.

But I will hope continually, and will praise you yet more and more;

Psalm 71:14 (NKJV)

Always put your hope in God:

This is Christ's encouragement to us.

About the Author

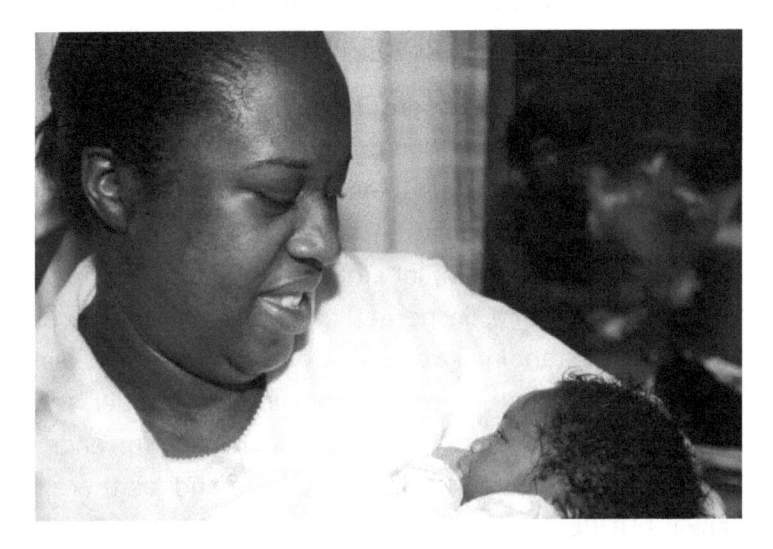

Maxine Mukuna lives in Birmingham, United Kingdom. Her professional career spans over 30 years, working in the health & social care field. Currently, she works as a Deputy Manager with people who have learning disabilities, as well as being a part-time administrator within her local church, Small Heath Church of God of prophecy, where she regularly attends.

Maxine appreciates her loving family, Mum and Dad, Pernella and Clariston King; Sisters Zena, Carol and Sharmaine; Brothers-in-law Rob and Shaun; Nieces and Nephews Dominique, Chanel, Kiarah, Kristin, O'shay, Marissa, Benjamin and Brianna.

HOPE

Through writing this book, Maxine has developed an urge to share her story with others, to encourage all that even during a terrible sense of loss, in God there is HOPE.

The loss of her only daughter Ruby, was something she did not imagine she would have to experience. That devastating pain took her to an all-time low in her life and she nearly lost her mind. In fact, she did not think she would ever smile again, let alone live and it broke her to a point where she desperately wanted to give up. Yet here she is, standing strong, as God had a different plan for her life. Today she encourages you, the reader, that regardless of what life throws at you, do not surrender, give up or give in. Keep fighting till the end, as there is always HOPE!

HOPE

WE PUBLISH BOOKS

PEACHES PUBLICATIONS

We Will Help You:
- Tell Your Story
- Become an Author
- Save You Time Writing

Our Services
Accountability Book Coaching
Silver Elite - Author's Starter Kit
Express Elite – Publish A Book In 4 Weeks
Gold Elite - Become A Publisher

Contact Us Today:
www.peachespublications.com
peachespublications@outlook.com
(+44) 07944 455 010